Sell Short

Sell Short

A SIMPLER, SAFER WAY TO PROFIT WHEN STOCKS GO DOWN

Michael Shulman

WILEY

John Wiley & Sons, Inc.

Published by John Wiley & Sons, Inc., Hoboken, New Jersey.
Published simultaneously in Canada.

For general information on our other products and services or for technical support, please contact our Customer Care Department within the United States at (800) 762-2974, outside the United States at (317) 572-3993 or fax (317) 572-4002.

Wiley also publishes its books in a variety of electronic formats. Some content that appears in print may not be available in electronic books. For more information about Wiley products, visit our web site at www.wiley.com.

Library of Congress Cataloging-in-Publication Data:
Shulman, Michael.
    Sell short : a simpler, safer way to profit when stocks go down / Michael Shulman.
        p.   cm.
    Includes index.
    ISBN 978-0-470-41233-6 (cloth)
        1. Short selling.   2. Stocks.   I. Title.
    HG6041.S488   2009
    332.63'228—dc22
                                                                2008048375

Printed in the United States of America.

10 9 8 7 6 5 4 3 2 1

To my wife, JJ, for her infinite patience, invaluable support, and the world's most loving red pen. And I promise, more to come.

Contents

Sell Short

Introduction

There is something almost sexy—if anything remotely related to investing and trading could be called or considered sexy—about shorting stocks. Just as the term "politics" often conjures up visions of smoke-filled rooms filled with faceless deal-making by men of power, shorting evokes images of men in bright suspenders with cigars and whiskey snifters discussing what company they should kill next on the stock market.

Ah, investing in the time of visual media.

I don't wear suspenders and I don't smoke cigars, yet I collect rare whiskeys and I short the hell out of stocks. Technically, I invest against stocks and markets and have made my subscribers obscene amounts of money since my newsletter service, *ChangeWave Shorts*, came into existence in the fourth quarter of 2006. My analytical approach is that of an investor—I stick to fundamentals; and my positions are those of a trader—a mix that has kept me and my subscribers ahead of Wall Street. This approach also kept me in the fray when the Securities and Exchange Commission (SEC) suspended the traditional shorting of financial stocks in September 2008. And that is what this book is all about—a marriage of fundamental investing and trading techniques to make spectacular profits on what the Street calls "the short side" of the market. The fundamentals tell me, and you, what is wrong with a company or market segment; the trading tool enables you to take maximum advantage of that weakness in a relatively short period of time. And, with shorting, time is on our side—a stock or segment may take six months or a year to rise 10 percent or 20 percent or 40 percent; that can all be given back on one day when bad news or a major catalyst tells investors something is wrong with the company they did not know of before.

You can short anything—stocks, bonds, ETFs, indices, futures—and you can use a variety of techniques: outright shorting by borrowing shares, buying puts, writing calls, writing spreads, and so

1

on. You can even short a raging bull market rally. All of this seems mysterious and unapproachable, but it is not. So-called experts like to hide behind jargon and charts that look more like the diagram of a new form of pasta rather than admit that shorting stocks is about making money on something that goes wrong—and spotting what is wrong is something all of us can do, right now.

This approach fits current trends in the market and among individual investors. Five years ago at a Money Show—a trade show for individual investors—when we asked several hundred subscribers to various ChangeWave services how many actively traded, the show of hands was 10 percent to 15 percent. When we asked that question in August 2008, the response was roughly 85 percent. The jargon and speed often linked to the term "trading" may make a more traditional investor take pause, but that should not be the case. Puts and ETFs—the two principal instruments used to short lousy companies and market segments—are as easy to buy and sell as most stocks. And when you marry weakening fundamentals to trading tools such as a put you create tremendous opportunities for short side profits. Trading is not hard—it may be new, and to a certain extent requires a bit more of your time—and when married to weakening fundamentals creates tremendous opportunities for short side profits.

In this book I will show you how to select a fundamentally weak—and weakening—company and stock, market segment, or index, independent of market conditions. I will then show you how to use a variety of trading techniques, depending on your tolerance of risk and your financial goals, on how to best go about making money when a dog of a stock finally goes down. Along the way I will use many examples from my service, including e-mail from subscribers—people just like you—on how and what they did, and the money they made.

This is not a trading system, nor is it a set of hard and fast rules for a particular kind of fundamental analysis. Rather it is a method geared to individual investors, financial advisors, and money managers unfamiliar with and (probably) uncomfortable with putting money to work on the dark side. This method works in a very unambiguous manner—in 2007, with the S&P up 3.7 percent, the average position in my short newsletter service, *ChangeWave Shorts*, was up 50 percent.

If you flip pages—before or after buying the book—do not be fooled by the language I have opted to use. I have tried very hard to avoid jargon, charts, complexity, and other tactics used by others to show how smart they are and how dumb the reader is. You are not dumb, you are very smart, having taken a critical step in your financial future or the future of your clients—you have decided to go short. You have been my guide in writing this book and it is designed to answer this question: What does the individual investor need to know to make money on the short side?

I have been writing for both institutional investors and individuals for seven years and the key to getting a point across is to imagine a dialogue with a subscriber or someone attending one of my seminars at a Money Show. As part of the preparation of this book I have not just imagined this dialogue but reached out to my subscribers, attendees at my seminars as well as hedge fund managers, advisors, stock brokers, and other money managers, not to mention the professionals at the Chicago Board of Options, ChicagoOne, the exchange for single stock futures, and two brokerages specializing in options trading, Options Express and ThinkorSwim. Critical input was given by Jerry Scheinman, managing director of Alcyone Capital. I have also solicited the input and advice from that media star and options guru, Jon Najarian of OptionsMonster; Bryan Perry, money manager and editor of *The ChangeWave Tactical Trader;* and the founder of ChangeWave and the man with the best understanding of what drives individual investors perhaps to be found anywhere, Tobin Smith. I also want to thank all the people at ChangeWave who put up with me every day: Dave Durham, Chris Marett, Howie Present, Chip French, Dawn Pennington, Val Maczak, Greg Tucker, Kim Gerdes, and Emily Norris.

But the most important contributor was my toughest critic and greatest supporter, my too long patient wife, Jackie Judd, a far better writer than I could ever hope to be (with two Emmys and various other awards to prove it) and a never-ending source of whatever I needed when I needed it.

And my thanks to you for buying my book, and if you are still debating whether to buy this book I ask you to consider the following story. In October 2007 I noticed lots of coupons at casual dining restaurants—being marketed and being used—and asked our survey group at ChangeWave to do a restaurant survey. They did, and using a simple set of survey data from ChangeWave Research, plus third-party data available to anyone, and a few tax deductible dining experiences, led me to recommend the shorting of Ruby Tuesday in the fall of 2007. A couple of months later my conservative subscribers were up about 500 percent, the aggressive ones 1,500 percent. And they could even check out my arguments and enjoy the salad bar at the same time—my teenage sons prefer the ribs or mini hamburgers. Did I think Ruby Tuesday was going out of business? Nope. Did I think Wall Street did not understand how their business was going to be hit by competition and the recession not yet called a recession? You bet. Not so complicated after all.

You can do it—put your doubts away—find your inner contrarian that has made you money on the long side, and come join me on the dark side where the brightest profits can be found. Now.

CHAPTER 1

The Schadenfreude Component of Your Portfolio

German is a rich language that has many expressions and words that do not translate with the vigor and depth they hold in their original form. One is schadenfreude, the German word for "taking delight in the misery of others."

In this book, I am going to teach you how to profit (and at parties and other places you can brag, revel) from financial schadenfreude. My definition of schadenfreude is simple—"making delightful profits in the misery of stocks." I know this sounds awful, and is a play on words, but successful shorting is nothing short of fun. You may be happy when a company has great earnings or gets an FDA approval for a new wonder drug to treat bald men with erectile dysfunction but there is nothing like the rush when some dog of a company misses big time, or does something else stupid and blows up completely . . . especially if you have money in the right place at the right time.

I was sitting on the Washington set of Fox Business News when Bear Stearns began the last stage of its volcanic meltdown on Friday, March 14, 2008. My recommendation to short Bear was just seven trading days old. It was about 9:55, the producer was speaking in my ear and giving me a five-minute warning; I looked up at the monitor and saw the stock was absolutely melting. I pulled out my Blackberry, typed an alert to subscribers, sent it to my editor, and closed the position with a 287 percent gain. And when the anchor began asking me about Bear, about seven minutes later,

I was on fire—in a true state of financial schadenfreude. Why? Because I was right—Bear was a dog, a dog among many Wall Street dogs, and it had just completely blown up.

Why did this feel so good?

Because **stocks fall a lot faster on bad news than they climb on good news,** excepting a little biotech getting a major FDA approval or a company being acquired at a ridiculous price. Short positions work a lot faster—when they work. In fact, I closed Bear too early. The following Monday the stock went from $25 to $2 and the puts I closed would have been up 800 percent. Many of my subscribers did hang on and made that 800 percent in less than two weeks.

Growth in the Shorting of Stocks

Shorting is now a common occurrence and variations such as naked shorting have been in the headlines for many months. In mid-2007 the SEC ended the uptick rule, and one year, lots of volatility, and $100 billion in shares later, shorting became as natural to many investors as going long. In the past years dozens of Exchange Traded Funds (ETFs) designed to short (or double short, more on that later) have come into being. Put volume has exploded in the last year and, the last indicator and my favorite indicator of the growing acceptance of shorting, my newsletter *ChangeWave Shorts* has added a great many subscribers. It isn't just the profit opportunities presented in a volatile and down market—it is people coming to understand that there are two sides of a trade and what is so wrong about playing the downside of a stock movement? If you have never shorted a stock or bought a put, and are about to do so, you are not an explorer or pioneer—you are an early settler on a new frontier.

What sent you to this frontier? You want to make money and fast profits based on great trades.

The Contrarian View

Most investors and traders going short are contrarians—they do well going against the grain. You may not view yourself this way but you have already bought the book so take another look in the mirror. What really is a contrarian? It is the person looking at the bounce in homebuilding stocks in January 2008 as analysts cried a bottom must be near—the contrarians drove around in their cars and saw abandoned home sites and more and more for sale signs. It is the trader saying I don't care if the stock is down 50 percent and that is a historical trough, the damned restaurant is giving away coupons left and right and the parking lot is empty most of the time. And it is the newsletter writer—moi—who hears analysts saying Citigroup will never cut its dividend but spends time with überanalyst Meredith Whitney (totally brilliant, now with Oppenheimer), reads the SEC documents and says those guys at Citigroup are toast (a formal analytical term for being in deep trouble), the other analysts are wrong. Thirty-five points to the downside later, the position had made a great deal of money showing the great value of being in early, ahead of the herd on Wall Street.

If you have only invested on the long side, remember that many great long side investors are also contrarians—a fellow by the name of Buffett calls it value investing but the deep value he finds is only found in stocks other people hate, making him the ultimate contrarian.

The corollary to being a contrarian is to **avoid the crowd**. The madness of crowds. The momentum players. The headline traders. This does not mean you avoid a great opportunity because other people may see the same thing—or if it has downside momentum—I just think you should avoid going short simply because momentum is there. I know, some of the great trading systems of the past few years are built around momentum indicators—go for it if you will—but that is not what true shorting is about. Momentum trading is agnostic to the long or the short side and because the relative value of indicators changes as the market changes, momentum systems work and do not work based on market conditions. On the other hand, going short is about lousy companies—and lousy companies and declining market segments—as measured by fundamentals. Momentum passes; fundamentals are forever.

Instead, think contrarian, against the crowd, against and ahead of wrong Wall Street expectations. Ah, yes, those famous Wall Street expectations. If you keep reading, I will show where and how to gauge those expectations to better measure your own, hopefully contrarian and therefore profitable views. The bottom line: There is a great deal of money to be made investing against the Four Hs that drive Wall Street: headlines, hysteria, hype, and hope.

Getting Started—Where in Your Portfolio?

What percentage of your portfolio should you allocate to shorting? Sorry, the question is not that simple. The funds you use for shorting stocks should be from your trading account and/or high risk capital—and that means it lies somewhere between 0 percent and 100 percent of your capital. When allocating capital, remember, you are not shorting the market, you are shorting lousy companies or lousy market segments that will fall regardless of or in spite of the market.

Getting started involves certain tasks:

- Determine what part of your portfolio will fund short investing.
- Determine what percentage of your capital goes to the short side.
- Determine how big each position will be.

I cannot and should not recommend to you how much money should be in the high risk or trading part of your portfolio. That being said, I ask you to look at the market itself as an asset subject to traditional asset allocation. What exactly do I mean? Traditional portfolio allocation says to diversify your portfolio along traditional lines—small cap, big cap, aggressive growth, domestic markets, foreign markets, emerging markets, income stocks, and so on. What is missing from traditional asset allocation formulas is the market itself. The market is always there; trading is always going on; there is a potential winner and loser for each trade; the trading of the market generates huge revenues every day. So consider the playing of the downside as playing the market itself, and this is a new slice of the asset allocation pie.

The first task is to determine where the capital you use to short stocks comes from—what part of your portfolio. One view is since you short a stock based on fundamentals, using the same logic as going long, you should use any funds you currently allocate toward buying equities. Another view is that since I am recommending you use puts—and, as you will see, without sell stops in most situations— you should only be using high risk or trading funds for shorting stocks. My view: **Start with funds you would normally allocate toward the higher risk component** of your portfolio, funds from a trading account, or funds you are currently using to trade options. As you get comfortable with the process, you can add funds from other parts of your portfolio as long as you remember puts can expire worthless.

The second task is to determine how much of your portfolio—your high risk funds—goes to the short side. It all depends on the opportunity. But since my first rule is to play defense, and the second is to wait for the great trade, it is best if each position is no more than 5 percent of the capital you have allocated for the short side, preferably less. Since you are shorting lousy companies, markets, or market segments, each judged to be going down for unique reasons, your decision to invest is based on the opportunity, not on a portfolio allocation mechanism, or some abstract decision about how the general market is moving. If you follow my lead, you don't or should not really care, except in extreme circumstances, where the market is going. You are exploiting an individual opportunity to make a profit, end of story.

Apart from this advice, **always let common sense take over**. Many successful investors and traders balance their portfolios with short positions in recognition that there is as much bad news and downside weakness in equities, bonds, and markets as there is upside. Warren Buffet does not short stocks but he made a massive bet against the U.S. dollar with a variety of investing instruments, in essence creating a short position against the greenback. If he can go short to exploit an opportunity or to provide some balance to his holdings, you can as well.

When to Short?

Your delight, your profits, your early retirement, your ridiculous case of wine—they come from being agnostic about the direction of the market and being right about a stock or market segment when most other investors are wrong.

When should you short a stock? While each trader has his own preferences for going short or long, several rules of thumb will help you get started and ultimately drive how you spot potential opportunities.

- **You short when you see bad news and disaster coming for a specific company or market segment, not based on a view**

of the overall direction of the market. Ahead of most of the folks on Wall Street. The bad news? Starbucks lowering guidance; the FDA reining in Amgen's drugs; Apple destroying Palm with the iPhone; and so on. All of these happened in the real world and all happened with the market going up.

- **You short when a great opportunity arises based on both the underlying fundamentals**—negative fundamentals—and a lack of unfavorable short-term technical indicators, which is different than looking for favorable indicators. This is different—far different—than looking for favorable technical indicators to initiate a trade.
- **Your best trade, the perfect trade is when the great opportunity—the weakening company—lies within another great opportunity—the sliding or crashing market segment.** The Bear Stearns meltdown is a great example of the near perfect trade.

My last point—you don't make a trade because you have not traded in a week or it is time to pay for Redskin season tickets (maybe for Giants season tickets, not the Redskins)—**you wait and wait and make a trade because it is a compelling opportunity**. Not when the market is going down or up, but when you find yourself with a compelling story Wall Street does not yet see.

Swing for the Fences

You are not in this game for a 10 percent pop over six months—you are in it for far more—and for this reason you also have higher risk. My method for creating and managing short positions has two elements: minimizing risk while swinging for home runs, not singles or doubles. Yes, you should cash out when all you can make is single or double but **the creation of a position should have an initial goal of hitting a home run—a position that doubles**. This approach creates risks—shorts can run away from you, puts can expire worthless—and this risk/reward ratio is what you need to keep in mind when shaping your commitment to short positions. You should take profits in the misery of others—but you should not make yourself miserable while doing it.

Speaking of balance, I am recommending, in the upcoming chapters, a fairly unbalanced approach to making profits. You will see that I urge you to be extremely patient, wait for great opportunities, and to look for home runs. And once you invest in these opportunities, you have to wait out volatility and movements against your position if you are still convinced your logic is sound going forward.

This method follows the practice and the words of many great traders and investors who have shown or told us three things: They made their most money when they stuck to their beliefs, even through tough times and volatility; they played their hand hard when profits appeared; and they told themselves to be disciplined and patient, there is always another trade or investment. Always. When things are looking great, people go long on a stock; when things look bad, they can go short. But there is no compelling need to make any investment or trade if it is not a great one—there is always another opportunity. Always. And the inverse means you do not chase things, you do not invest because you are restless or you need to make a car payment—you invest, you go short, because it is a great opportunity to make a very large profit.

The 5 Percent Solution (Preferably 3 Percent)

The flip side of all this preachiness about hitting home runs and waiting for great opportunities is the need to play defense and to be careful how you allocate your risk capital to one position. Many of you already have systems or rules in place—use them, do not change them because you are shorting a stock with a put. If you are new or undisciplined and do not have these rules for yourself, keep it simple—**never put more than 5 percent of your high risk or trading capital toward any one trade and less than 5 percent is preferable**. You may want to overweight some positions but you should never underweight a position; that means you are uncertain, which means you should not be making the investment.

You may think limiting your positions to this size will limit profits. It may—but the first rule is to do no harm, play defense, limit losses, and preserve capital. We are swinging for home runs, and you need a lot of at bats to get your fair share of home runs.

As part of limiting risk the 5 percent solution is not enough. You also need to be mindful of something people often forget—**you need to establish links between positions**. What does that mean? Well, if you got real jazzed seeing Bear Stearns blow up and quickly established 10 positions in banks, any big exogenous move—such as a lifeline to Fannie and Freddie, the suspension of shorting financial stocks, the bailout package, all government moves—could temporarily hit all 10 positions and they will trade as if they are one giant oversized position. There is nothing wrong in having more than one position in a market segment, but you need to make sure you are not accidentally overweight in one area due to correlations you may not have seen when you first created the position.

You also need to keep capital in reserve to make sure that, if the going gets good and the position is running, you can put more kerosene on the fire. I will discuss managing positions at much greater length in Chapter 11. And don't be arrogant; managing short positions, specifically put positions, is quite a different exercise, especially when using a fundamental approach, than other things you may have tried before. So keep reading.

Conclusion

The profits you make from short side positions typically happen faster than profits to be made from stocks moving up. The best way to do this is through puts—and with the use of a trading instrument that can expire worthless, you need to manage risk as tightly as you can, playing defense first and swinging for the fences only when the great trade is in front of you. And you need to accept the home run and take it off the table when you hit your goals.

Let me give you an example: In September 2008 I predicted that after Lehman the next to go would be WAMU and then Wachovia. This happened— and I closed the position in Wachovia the day before it totally blew up. The position more than doubled— and I closed it not willing to risk profits in the face of potential exogenous events, in this case government action, that might take these profits away. The next trading day the bulk of Wachovia was sold via the FDIC to Citigroup and the stock blew up. I left profits on the table—but I did not care. This discipline is what you need to succeed, consistently, when using put positions. Please remember—**there is always another great trade out there for the patient investor**.

Q1. If I have an existing system for sizing a position, should I still start with your 5 percent solution?

Yes and no. Yes, if something is working stick with it. No if that system or set of rules is for something other than high risk or option positions. Systems for allocating capital to individual positions that are longer term or equities are not appropriate for managing higher risk put positions.

Q2. How do you define home run?

Profits are in the eye of the beholder—but in my service I establish put positions with leverage that can get me to a double: a 100 percent gain—a doubling of your initial investment—if the underlying stock moves the way I believe it will. I have closed positions with modest gains, others with gains as high as 287 percent; no set of rules or targets should lock you in. I use the term home run as part of an overall approach of conserving capital but going for big winners, not a series of small winners.

Q3. I understand an individual position can go down while the market is going up. But do you really believe you can consistently make money from short positions in an up or bull market?

Yes. It may sound simplistic but you just need to select a series of positions based on their own merits, which should succeed independent of almost anything but a roaring bull. And I mean a roaring, irrational bull that lasts more than a few weeks, the kind we have only seen once in the past 20 years.

Q4. I have made the most money from trading with momentum. You preach being a contrarian. Should I stop here?

No. As I wrote, contrarian and momentum are not necessarily opposites. You would need to follow my method—core fundamentals plus technical indicators—and then add your own flavor by investing in positions that have an additional indicator, some form of momentum. Several of my more successful picks in banking in the first half of 2008—notably Citigroup and Bank of America—had already come down a great deal, hit a temporary bottom as value investors thought they were cheap, and I urged subscribers to go against this view and buy puts. The long-term trend was down, the current opinion was positive, the contrarian view was to go against the value investors and this proved to be highly successful.

Rules

- Stocks fall much faster on bad news than they climb on good news.
- Avoid the crowd.
- Start with funds you would normally allocate toward the higher risk component of your portfolio.
- Always let common sense take over.
- You short when you see bad news and disaster coming for a specific company or market segment, not based on a view of the overall direction of the market.
- You short when a great opportunity arises based on the underlying fundamentals.
- Your best trade, the perfect trade is when the great opportunity—the weakening company—lies within another great opportunity, the sliding or crashing market segment.
- You wait and wait and make a trade because it is a compelling opportunity.
- The creation of a position should have an initial goal of hitting a home run—a position that doubles.
- Never put more than 5 percent of your high risk or trading capital toward any one trade and less than 5 percent is preferable.

CHAPTER

How Shorting Works

Shorting appears to be complex and therefore out of the range of individual investors. That view is nonsense. At the most macro of levels, shorting is making an investment on the premise that a stock, market, or market segment will go down. This is exactly the same principle as investing on the long side. As you drill down into more tactical issues, it almost stays this simple.

I prefer to categorize shorting as actually investing against a company and its stock, or a market, or some other investment instrument. You will see why shortly.

There are several ways to invest against a company or market, all based on the simple reality that it takes two to tango—successful shorting requires two opinions, two beliefs, two sets of actions by investors—someone thinks an equity is going up and you think it is going down. Better still if most people think it is going up and you play the role of the contrarian.

So, what exactly is shorting? There are several flavors worth exploring.

- Traditional Shorting—Borrower Beware
- Shorting with Puts—Limiting Exposure
- Other Methods—Naked Calls, Naked Puts, Naked Shorting

Traditional Shorting—Borrower Beware

The oldest and most traditional form of shorting a stock involves the borrowing of shares of a company at one price (preferably a higher price) and repaying the loan with shares purchased at a lower price.

When Did It Start?

Some financial historians believe the first well-known and therefore notorious short seller of stocks was a fellow named Isaac Le Maire. He was a wealthy and successful merchant in Amsterdam who at the beginning of the seventeenth century shorted stocks, including the powerhouse Dutch East India Company, these stocks being traded on arguably the world's first true stock market, the Dutch stock exchange. After a major crash in 1610, the good burghers did what all authorities do: They regulated in favor of ever rising markets and outlawed short selling.

You go to a nationally owned restaurant, find the food terrible, the service indifferent, and other customers using discount coupons everywhere. You decide to short the stock. Next day you call your broker—yes, you should probably use a phone, not a mouse and laptop—and ask if they hold shares or can find shares of this company. She says yes, plenty are available, and then the fun starts. You borrow 1,000 shares, the current price of the stock being $20 a share. You immediately sell the shares and that money is put into a margin account you have set up for the purpose of shorting and nothing else. Some or all of that cash is tied up as collateral and will suffice to cover your position if the stock goes up a bit depending on your broker's requirements. However, if the stock goes up a lot—in this case, with your broker's rules, if it hits $30 or more—you start getting margin calls. And for every dollar the stock goes up you will need to put up 50 cents in collateral.

Other things to consider:

- When you borrow the shares, you pay interest to the brokerage house for this loan, and the harder the shares are to find, the higher the interest rate, and I have seen examples of 20 percent interest per annum.
- You may collect dividends, but you also pay them out to the person or persons you borrowed the shares from.

- If you make the mistake of co-mingling your long and short positions in the same account, and the short position starts going the wrong way, your broker can and will liquidate your long positions to cover margin calls.

Is this a good way to invest against a company and stock? Yes and no. Yes if you are a professional or institutional investor; no if you are an individual investor. Institutional investors are much better able to handle the margin calls and financial risks associated with the open-ended liability created by a traditional short position. You can do the math: If you short a stock at $20, and someone buys the company at $100, you are out five times your original investment. That is not the kind of liability any individual investor should face.

Yes, I just said in most cases individual investors should not short stocks through the borrowing of shares. There is a chapter on shorting stocks if you disagree, but I always urge individual investors to use puts.

Let me give you a concrete and horrifying example. I also write about biotech stocks and liked a company called Sirtris Pharmaceuticals. Many people did not, and after a successful IPO (Initial Public Offering) the stock lingered with the number of shares held short growing every day. Let's imagine on Thursday, April 22, sometime before the close, some short side investor who disliked Sirtris opened a new short position at about $12.25 a share—a small position, let's say 10,000 shares—and I am sure this was done by someone. The trader goes to bed, wakes up early—her dog being like my own, wanting a treat at sunrise—makes some coffee and checks the headlines. The coffee spills out onto the keyboard, it is burning hot, she is burned not just by the coffee but to the tune of 100 grand, her losses on Sirtris. How? British giant GlaxoSmithKline has offered Sirtris $22.50 a share and the company has accepted the bid.

One hundred grand. The original goal of this money manager was to make a 25 percent gain in a few weeks—she saw the stock going from $12.25 to $9.75–$10. Could she have played this position another way?

Yes, she could have bought a put and either minimized losses or made a lot of profit.

Shorting with Puts—Limiting Exposure

A second way to short stocks is to use put options contracts, forever-more (in this book) called puts. These contracts are the right to put the stock to a buyer at a fixed price at a date in the future. They are essentially a bet that a stock will go down. If you own a put, and you keep it through expiration, and the stock is at $20 and the put you hold has a strike price of $25, you can buy the stock at $20 and put it to the seller of the put at $25. In reality, puts are typically trading and hedging tools and only a minority of puts are exercised—most individual investors sell winning or losing put positions before expiration.

Let us go back to the Sirtris acquisition. Let's say that instead of shorting the stock the hedge fund trader bought puts that expired in July—a $15 put costing roughly $3.10 (imaginary but proximate numbers). The cost? To control 10,000 shares she needed to buy 100 put contracts—100 shares controlled per contract—so she would have spent roughly $30,000. If the stock had gone to the target price—$9.75—she would have made roughly $25,000, the same amount of money she would have made from direct shorting of the stock. And if the stock did not move, the puts could have been sold for $2.75 the day before they expired and the loss would have been $0.40 a share, $40 a contract, or $4,000. With the acquisition by Glaxo, she lost the whole $31,000—a lot less than the $100,000 she did lose.

I have gotten ahead of myself with terminology and thinking but I am leading you to the most important point in this entire book: **it is much safer and saner to short stocks using puts than to actually short a stock.** And as we get into it—the next chapter is all about puts—you will also see the inverse of protecting against losses—you can preserve capital more effectively and generate larger profits faster with puts than by the outright shorting of a stock.

Other Methods—Getting Naked, Going Broke

Yup, time for what I call financial porn—naked shorting and naked calls. These techniques are, in my opinion, the moral equivalent of pornography—they degrade buyer and seller. Naked shorting and the writing of naked calls are techniques used by speculators to short a stock without investing capital in the position, and naked shorting is, for the most part, against SEC regulations.

A naked short is the shorting of a stock without actually borrowing and selling the shares, what the SEC calls "affirmatively determined to exist." This practice is illegal. When a real short is underway, traders can either borrow shares or determine shares are available to be borrowed before they sell it short. A naked short is a position where the trader never takes possession of the shares and sells them, depressing the price, but does not complete the trade at settlement since the trader never took possession of the shares. Naked shorts are best revealed in data on failed-to-deliver trades. In 2007, the SEC added regulations to close existing loopholes. That being said, the prohibition on naked shorting was barely enforced and led to dramatic action against naked shorting of financial stocks in July 2008.

While doing research for this book, I had a wonderful conversation with a former floor trader in Chicago and he explained one method used by traders to execute a naked short position. The trader gets online—sometimes literally—for shares to borrow. She is at the back of the line. She is then told the shares will soon be available to borrow, and then when it is her turn to collect she says, oops, gotta go to the ladies' room or get a Starbucks, and she goes further back in the line. But she has executed the short, sold the shares in anticipation of reaping a quick profit with no intention of delivering those shares at settlement.

Naked shorting allows speculators to quickly hit a stock—traders doing this dump shares, obviously, that they have borrowed, or sort of borrowed, or claimed to have borrowed—and is a really nasty practice. It is frightening how little the SEC does to enforce its own rules.

Naked Shorting and the Great Headlines of 2008

Naked shorting became a buzzword—a buzz expression?—on CNBC, Fox Business, and Jay Leno in the summer of 2008 when the SEC grandly announced they were banning naked shorting in financial stocks—certain financial stocks, not all financial stocks. Those of us who have been around a bit knew the SEC had, several years before, put in place regulations banning naked shorting. But, like many government agencies, had neglected to enforce their own rules. In July 2004 the SEC published a rule stating clearinghouses should take action against naked short sellers 10 days after their trade fails to clear, meaning that they never borrowed the stock and therefore could not deliver it as sold. Under political pressure during the financial crisis, the SEC, four years later, in July of 2008, said it would not only enforce this rule but would initiate a ban on short selling in financial stocks, triggering a massive relief rally.

A naked put or call is the sale of an option without owning the underlying stock. The most aggressive form of shorting may be the sale of naked calls—you sell people the right to buy a stock at a price in the future; yet you don't own the stock—since you are assuming the price of the stock will be less than the price in the call contract. This is a common, and legal, practice among many aggressive traders looking to short thinly traded stocks with hard-to-find shares to short.

Avoid doing this because naked calls can also wipe traders out. Imagine that a struggling software company keeps failing to find a marketing partner, is burning cash, and its stock is going down—but it is too small to easily short; every attempt you make to locate the stock fails. So you write naked calls with a $2.50 strike price. This itty bitty company is selling for around $0.50 a share and you sell calls that you assume will expire worthless in two months for 10 cents. The company cuts a deal with an industry giant such as Microsoft or Oracle to market their product. The stock immediately runs up and the person who has bought the calls you sold exercises them around $2.50. You are out 25 times what you were paid for the call. Not a good risk, not now, not ever.

Conclusion

Shorting can be profitable—very profitable—in any of its forms but individual investors should begin and preferably stick with shorting through the use of puts. If there is one thing I hope to accomplish with this book it is to bring this point home—that puts are where it is at and **puts are inherently less risky than borrowing shares** and waiting at home for the phone to ring with a margin call. There are also great advantages to using puts, which I will explore in detail in later chapters, namely leverage as well as the ability to roll a position—to play one company to the downside several times through a series of put positions.

Q&A

Q1. I am confused. This book is about shorting. Yet you urge individuals to avoid shorting stocks and to buy puts instead. Is there any situation where you recommend shorting a stock outright?

Yes, with some qualifications you can find in Chapter 8. If you believe you are qualified and have the capital, well, it's your life, I just

(Continued)

would never do it myself or recommend an individual short stock. But if you must, many smaller stocks do not have put options or put options are available but illiquid. In this case, shorting a stock may be a safer alternative. Hot stocks with charts in free fall—the trend line looks like a ski slope—are also difficult to short in that put premiums get expensive and spreads (the difference between the Bid price and the Ask price) can be ridiculous. Outright shorting of a stock may make more economic sense in these situations.

Q2. Naked calls seem to be a good way to short an illiquid stock that does not have attractively priced puts or whose puts have too little liquidity. Are they really that risky?

In the summer of 2008 a little microcap, Isolagen, trading around 50 cents a share, announced strong clinical trial results for a new treatment and said it would proceed to ask the FDA for approval to bring it to market. An hour after the announcement the stock was trading at $2.50 and change—which, coincidentally, was the strike price of the lowest priced call you could buy—or in this case, sell—in the stock. Millions of shares changed hands, and the stock settled down to about $1.30 in a day or so. A lot of sellers of naked calls got bruised, big time, having sold $2.50 calls for pennies and then having to come up with $2.50 a share to cover these calls.

Rules

In most cases individual investors should not short stocks through the borrowing of shares. It is much safer and saner to short stocks using puts than to actually short a stock.

CHAPTER

The Case for Puts

As you might have guessed, I prefer and will focus on the use of puts to invest against stocks, markets, and other investment instruments. If you have more interest in traditional shorting, well, read this and then read Chapter 8. Then come back and read this chapter again.

If you are new to trading puts, you may find the information I present valuable. It is nice to know what you are buying and selling, right? And if you are experienced in buying and selling puts, well, consider this information to be a brief refresher on what puts really are—the best way to short a company with weakening fundamentals.

So, let's begin with some definitions and explanations first for the first-time put buyer.

What Exactly Is a Put?

A put is a legal contract obligating the buyer to accept delivery and pay for a stock at a fixed price on or before a fixed date sometime in the future. If John Smith buys one put contract—this controls 100 shares—of Pocahontas Clothing, and the put has what is called a strike price (more on that later) of $20, and the shares fall to $10, well, John is stuck, he has to buy and pay $20 for the shares if the seller exercises the put. The exercise of the put—the actual selling of the stock to the put buyer—is at the discretion of the seller.

One put contract controls 100 shares of the underlying stock. These are trading instruments used by most traders and investors to invest against a stock. A put has four major components or characteristics:

1. **The strike price:** This is the price the seller of the put will pay for the stock if the buyer of the put exercises the right to put the stock. A $20 put is just that—the right to sell a stock for $20 to the seller of that put.
2. **The expiration date:** This is the last date the right to put the stock can be exercised. In the United States, in theory, a buyer of a put can exercise the put anytime before the expiration date. In Europe and for many index options, puts can only be exercised on the expiration date.
3. **Liquidity:** This defines the number of put contracts outstanding and the number of contracts traded each day. When selecting a put to buy when creating a short position, liquidity is important for the greater the liquidity, the easier and less expensive it is to enter or exit a position. Liquidity is the central ingredient in determining the spread or the difference between the bid and the ask price for a put contract.
4. **Volatility:** The technical definition of volatility is "how much does that sucker bounce around"—how much does a put move up or down in the context of market conditions and in the context of movement in the underlying stock.

Puts typically have expiration dates less than a year from the day they become available. **Longer term puts are called LEAPS** (Long Term Equity AnticiPation Securities) and are available for a limited number of equities, roughly 500 as well as a dozen or so indices. If held for more than one year they enjoy long-term capital gains treatment by the IRS.

Pricing of Puts

The true fair market value of a put is the price of the last sale of a put. Yeah, I know, not very useful, but the pricing of all options is something of a black art regardless of what quants, geeks, and Nobel Prize winners have to say about it.

The pricing of puts is still a black art although a formal method with the formidable name of Black–Scholes is now the standard used by most pricing models, software, Wall Street analysts, and stock market soothsayers. Advanced traders find a good deal of utility in using Black–Scholes predictors as a benchmark and do trading based on deviations from these benchmarks. Many online and software pricing models use their work as a basis for providing users with an estimate at fair value of an option. That being said, Black–Scholes is mostly irrelevant for what you need to do when creating put positions as we are more interested in the fundamental performance of a company and the matching performance of its stock. The bottom line—**what you need to know to make you comfortable with the price of a put is fairly simple**.

First, a brief set of definitions I use—specifically **in-the-money versus out-of-the-money puts.** An in-the-money put is literally in the money. An example would be a $20 put on a stock that is currently trading for $15. An out-of-the-money put would be the inverse—a $15 put for a stock currently trading for $20. These are common terms investors sometimes confuse with profits and losses—they simply represent whether the stock has fallen below the strike price of the put.

Another word you will see a lot of and need to know is "premium." **The option or put premium** is used in two ways by traders: as the term for the price of a put and to describe that part of a put over and above the fair value of that put. Many professionals will cringe at this definition but for the purposes here it will suffice. If a stock is $20 and a $15 put is priced at $1, the put is said to have $6 worth of premium. On the other hand many often call the price of an option its premium. The **spread** on a put option is the difference between the **bid price**—what someone is willing to pay for the put—and the **ask price**, what someone is willing to sell that same put for in the market.

Classic analysis says there are **three components that drive the price of a put. I disagree and have added a fourth**—we are not doing classic analysis, we are simply trying to make money.

1. **The core or intrinsic value** of a put is that part of a put price that is in the money. This is the intrinsic value of an option, and the way I use this term it applies only to puts that are in the money—a put with a strike price higher than the current price of the stock. A January 2010 $30 put on Home Depot has an intrinsic value of $3.63 as I write this. The stock is currently selling for $26.37. Not too hard to estimate this variable!

2. **The time value of an option** is the value to a purchaser of the time between the date of the purchase and the expiration date of the put. Calculating this one is a bit harder—what is the time value of a particular put bedevils many analysts and, forgetting theories and formulas, it is a value set by the market and the market's expectations of where a stock and therefore an option is headed. More than any other metric, time value will give you a sense of what the market sees as the future of a stock and when this future occurs.

3. **The volatility of an option is contributing more and more to how puts are priced** in the market—the more volatile an option and the underlying security, the higher the price and the larger the spread between the bid and the ask for the option. There are too many people saying too many things about how to play with beta and how to make money on puts. This is not about that. Stock volatility is measured in a fancy term called beta—and option volatility, as reflected in changes in the premium, is measured by something called **vega.** Ah, jargon. What you need to know about volatility is simple: a high beta, highly volatile stock is going to have put options that have higher premiums, a higher potential return, and is going to bounce around day to day unless the stock moves in a straight line down. And puts with a higher vega will also have higher premiums for the same reasons. Volatility is often but not always linked to the volatility of the underlying security. Volatility in a put not seen in the underlying stock indicates speculators know something—or think they know something—is going to happen by a certain date and is an indicator investors need to be aware of when considering a position.

4. **The liquidity of a put is typically measured by contracts outstanding,** an important factor in choosing a put. **An illiquid put costs more than a liquid one**—the seller can command a greater premium from the buyer. In options markets the rule of thumb is the seller always has the advantage. When there are not that many contracts around, the spread between the Bid (what you want to pay) and the Ask (what the seller wants) widens. Back in the good old days before online trading I traded options through a broker who would go down to the floor, and I could hear the brokers cursing as the Ask kept moving away on thinly traded puts.

A few years ago, when Claritin, an antihistamine, was about to go generic, I discovered a small company called Albany Molecular Research (AMRI) received royalties from Allegra, a competitor. I looked at AMRI's financial statements and realized more than 100 percent of their profits were from Allegra royalties; the rest of the company was losing money. I went to buy puts and made the mistake of chasing them, buying them too high and selling them too soon because I had committed too much capital to the trade and it was making me nervous. My mistake was not being aware of the problems with illiquidity and managing to get around them by buying fewer contracts at a higher price.

When I look at liquidity, I like to see at least **7,500 contracts** outstanding across all expiration dates, preferably more, and at least **1,500 on one expiration date**. That is not exactly a lot of liquidity and you will see larger spreads at this level, but this enables us to include more stocks in our shorting universe.

Advantages of Puts

The term "expiration" often puts fear into the mind (and heart) of a first-time buyer of an option, put, or call. This fear is misplaced—puts present great advantages to individuals, especially to short-side investors smart enough to avoid the unlimited financial exposure inherent in a traditional short position. Here are the critical advantages of puts:

- **Puts have less risk, a key factor in preserving capital.** The key to shorting is to preserve capital and go for home runs; using puts is the best way to accomplish both goals. Let's go back to the Sirtris example. Let's say that instead of shorting the stock, the hedge fund trader bought puts that expired in July, a $15 put costing roughly $3.10 (imaginary but proximate numbers). The cost? To control 10,000 shares she needed to buy 100 put contracts—100 shares controlled per contract—so she would have spent roughly $30,000. If the stock had gone to the target price—$9.75—she would have made roughly $25,000, the same amount of money she would have made from direct shorting of the stock. And if the stock did not move, the puts could have been sold for $2.75 the day before they expired and the loss would have been 40 cents a share, $40 a contract, or $4,000. With the acquisition by

Glaxo, she would have lost the whole $35,000, a lot less than the $100,000 she did lose.

- **Puts require investors to put up less capital per opportunity.** As you saw in the example of Sirtris, a person using puts required far less capital to establish a position that could return the same dollar profit than someone shorting a stock outright. The ability to use less capital per position gives an investor the ability to establish a larger number of short positions, spread risk, and create more opportunities for home runs.
- **Puts create more leverage** and this is a natural corollary to the need for less capital for a position as shown in Figure 3.1. Let's get away from Sirtris and look at another trade. In July 2008 it was time to short Wachovia. On July 23 the January 2009 $10 puts sold for $0.95 when the stock was trading at $17.65—and a buyer had six months for this position to play out and garner a double or 100 percent gain. Three days later the stock was at $14.50—and the news was bad enough that the premiums on the puts had expanded rapidly and hit $2.05. Time to sell—and capture a 116 percent gain in three days. If you had shorted the stock, you would have had an 18 percent gain. As you read on you will see a walk through what I call a "rocket fueled trade" using a call option—the inverse of puts—on something called a double short ETF (love that jargon again) that returned 700 percent in two days based on a 10 percent move in one market segment. Got you interested? Keep reading.
- **Puts have a favorable risk/reward ratio, always the basis of a great trade.** At the end of a trade the most you can make by traditionally shorting a stock is a double and only if that company goes bankrupt. A trader can realize that size gain well before a company goes into bankruptcy and its stock hits zero by owning a put position without risking more than the initial capital used to create the trade. The bottom line is puts provide a much more favorable risk/reward ratio than traditional shorting.
- **Puts allow you to multiply your profit.** Rolling a position is the term I use for closing a position, taking a profit, and then buying another put that has a later expiration date or a different strike price, or both, on the same stock. I cannot state this

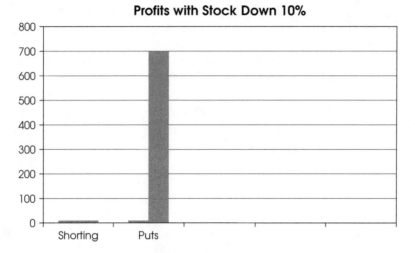

Figure 3.1   Puts versus Traditional Shorting

in a stronger fashion—**this is the single greatest advantage of using puts to execute a fundamental view of a stock**. If you short a stock in a traditional fashion, the most you can make is 100 percent of your investment—the company goes bankrupt and you never have to repay the loan of borrowed shares. Ah, what is 100 percent to folks like us? When you roll a position, you can make multiples of this kind of gain from the same movement in the stock price. For example, in the fall of 2007 the stock of Ruby Tuesday fell from $15.61 to $6.01 on January 11, 2008, a fall of 61 percent. During that period I recommended that subscribers buy, close, buy, close, buy, and close three sets of puts over time. The positions returned 100 percent, 177 percent, and 247 percent; compound them and you have an almost 15-fold increase in one fundamental view of one company, something you could not come close to approximating with a traditional short position.

- **Puts are ever more liquid as markets are seeing ever increasing trading in options/liquidity.** The shorting of stocks has exploded in the first year since the uptick rule was abandoned. More than $100 billion in stocks were shorted, a huge increase in a very short period of time. That being said, the issuing and use of puts has increased even faster. I estimate there are more than 2,500 stocks, ETFs, and equities mirroring market averages that are now liquid enough for individual investors to use to create short positions and enjoy adequate liquidity. On the day I wrote this section more than 2.1 million put contracts changed hands, and this was during vacation season.

Investors have new and better trading platforms that in turn have made the analyses of various puts, the management of trading accounts and portfolios, and the execution of trades far simpler than even two or three years ago. My first great option trade—May 1987—earned me a year's salary and was executed with a broker on the phone and a floor trader I actually got to speak to. No more. These trading platforms are typically provided by brokerage houses specializing in options trading such as OptionsExpress and ThinkorSwim.

Conclusion

The key to any trading—or investing for the long term—is the risk reward ratio of a position and puts offer, by far, the best risk reward ratio for short-side investors. The key is not to confuse the risk reward profile of an individual position—some may be high risk, others lower—with that of your entire trading account or short-side portfolio. This is where puts are so far superior to borrowing shares and selling them. I can think of only a few situations where you might consider shorting a stock in the traditional manner—for these see Chapter 8—and even then I would discourage you from doing so.

The bottom line: **When you think of going short, think puts**.

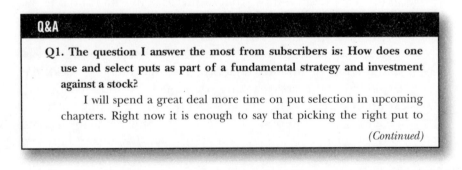

Q&A

Q1. The question I answer the most from subscribers is: How does one use and select puts as part of a fundamental strategy and investment against a stock?

I will spend a great deal more time on put selection in upcoming chapters. Right now it is enough to say that picking the right put to

(Continued)

support a fundamental and often longer-term view of a stock's decline is different than trying to make a quick trade and usually involves puts six months away from expiration or longer. Even though there is a good deal of time value embedded in the price, if you are truly ahead of the market with your view on fundamentals, the puts will increase in price not just because of declines in the underling stock but because more and more buyers who want puts will pay higher prices, expanding the premium. This is what happened in the example of Wachovia I gave earlier in this chapter. The bottom line: If your view of fundamentals is contrarian and catches on, premiums on the put will expand. Fundamentals always become exposed and drive stocks and eventually options and puts.

Q2. Do I need to open a special account just to buy and trade puts?

No, not at all. I occasionally buy puts through a human being known as a stock broker at a large brokerage house in addition to my online accounts. But some brokerage houses offer better platforms—either Web-based or software you put on your computer—that let you do a lot of things when looking at or trading puts. It all depends on how sophisticated you are as an investor or trader. One word of caution: If you open up a new account to trade options or just puts, check with the brokerage house on what their account minimums are for day- or short-term traders. Regulations have forced many brokerages to up minimum account size for some traders.

Rules

- Classical analysis says three components drive the price of a put—the core value, the time value, and volatility of that put. I believe there is a fourth—liquidity.
- The volatility of an option is contributing more and more to how puts are priced.
- An illiquid put costs more than a liquid one.
- Puts have less risk, a key factor in preserving capital.
- Puts require the investor puts up less capital per opportunity.
- Puts create more leverage.
- Puts have a favorable risk/reward ratio compared to traditional shorting.
- Rolling a position is the single greatest advantage of using puts to execute a fundamental view of a stock.

Prospecting for Gold in Fading Stocks

This chapter could be repeated at the beginning of each of the following chapters each covering a different kind of short position—a stock, a market segment, a market index, commodities, real estate, or foreign countries. Rather than repeat myself and drive you to desperation, **consider this chapter *the* chapter on prospecting** and I will change this method as needed for different categories of opportunities. **The key to successful shorting any part of the market is sticking to fundamentals**. That and remembering going short is no different than going long except you are aware that when bad news hits, a stock typically falls faster and deeper than when good news breaks. For instance, it took Fannie Mae many decades to climb to $100; the stock lost more than 90 percent of its value in less than a year.

The hardest thing for my subscribers—many of whom have made boatloads of profits from going long and are experienced investors—is reconciling a fundamental approach with a short-term trading tool, a put. The volatility of puts and LEAPS can drive you crazy even when they do not expire for 6, 12, or even 24 months. I preach, and sometimes I get e-mail saying enough already, stop preaching, but I preach anyway and what I preach is patience. It is the only solution to this problem—but the heart of what I do, and what you need to do, **when picking a target, is to act like an investor, not a trader**, and focus on fundamentals, and with that focus must come a concomitant commitment to patience.

That being said, I will ask you to **act like a trader when you create, manage, and exit a position**.

As a long-side investor you know what fundamentals drive a stock price up. Now you need to focus on what drives a stock price down. What makes a stock a lousy investment and therefore a place for you to make money?

Prospecting

The prospecting process is both similar and dissimilar from making a long-side pick. You need to look at fundamentals, use common sense, and practice all those other things advisors write up in platitudes for investors. This is a dissimilar process for shorting because of one major variable—**time**. First, short positions pay off more quickly as stocks typically fall faster on bad news than they climb on good news. Second, puts expire and their value decays a bit every day, making time a much more essential ingredient in selecting a position than in other types of investing.

The rules of prospecting for shorts are similar to those for developing a long position and begin with the individual psyche—individual discipline—rules far removed from numbers, charts, data, financial documents, and other material you would examine to determine the fundamental prospects of a company.

> **Patience—Waiting for Great Trade:** Speaking of time, the first awareness you should have of time is to put no time limits on establishing a position, **wait for the great trade to come to you**. Many people (and this often includes me) feel almost compelled to put some money to work. I lost $50,000 a couple of years ago buying Apple LEAPS. The stock ended up moving my way, but I rushed the position and closed it way too soon because I felt I had to do something and wanted to force myself out of what I had called "investing doldrums." To quote General Rommel when he was told the Allies had surprised everyone by landing at Normandy, "dumpf mir." Me, too.
>
> Great investments and trades are out there, and if you wait for the great ones, you will have more capital to use as the basis for making great profits. The absolute great trade worth waiting for, which is slowly taking place now but will not culminate until late 2010/early 2011 unless Wall Street

wakes up, is generic Lipitor. Lipitor is the best-selling drug in the world with $12 to $13 billion in sales, yet most of these sales, according to ChangeWave surveys and common sense, will go away when its patent does. Although this book is not about concrete recommendations, Pfizer and Lipitor are perfect examples of the great trade that is now happening in slow motion. So, just be patient.

The best way to prove this point is to examine what happened when Claritin went generic in the early part of this decade. If you were patient and had waited for this trade, you could have ignored most everything else. If you refer to Figure 4.1, which shows Schering Plough (SGP), the manufacturer of Claritin, you will see why I call it the trade of the decade. As you can see, the great slide went from roughly $60 to $15 with plenty of entry points—all based on the simplest of theories: Generic Claritin would whack branded Claritin and hit Schering Plough hard.

The great trade becomes the perfect, okay, *near* **perfect trade when you target a weakening company inside a weakening market segment**—think Citigroup in banking in the fall of 2007 and in 2008. As you can see in Figure 4.2, the segment, represented by an ETF called the XLF, went down and provided no support for Citigroup. It is ideal to look for waves of

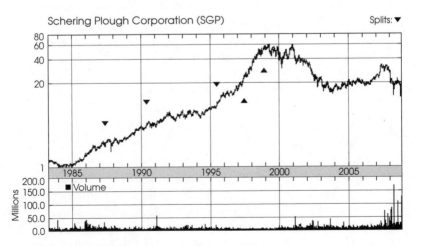

Figure 4.1   The Impact of Claritin

Source: CSI Data

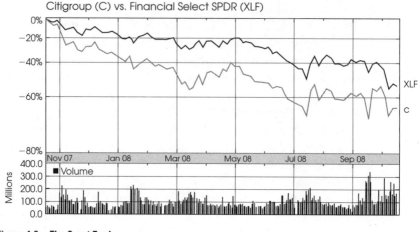

Figure 4.2   The Great Trade

Source: CSI Data

negative sentiment about a segment to support your negative view of an individual company. Positive sentiment will lead to money flowing into ETFs and other funds that focus on the segment and buy baskets of stocks—including bad ones. This point becomes more important every quarter as more money flows to segment ETFs and mutual funds.

Common Sense: Even without being an industry expert, or a subscriber to ChangeWave Research survey data on generic drugs, the question about setting up a short position in Schering Plough was simple: Would customers and, more importantly, insurance companies, pay three to six times as much for a medication for a routine illness (that had a lot of competition) simply for the brand name? My dog Sumo knows the answer to that one. Ditto for generic Lipitor. When you can buy Lipitor for $20 a month rather than $80, well, that is a good basis for a short. Especially when the drug is worth $12- to $13 billion or more than 25 percent of Pfizer's sales, and could be generating up to half their profits. Pfizer would have to introduce 10 blockbuster drugs by 2011 to replace the revenue it is likely to lose within a year or two of Lipitor going generic. *Always go with common sense,* and in this example about five minutes of reading says Pfizer will not be able to do it.

Keep Your Story (and Position) Simple: When the great trade is there, **don't get fancy**. Buy a put. Don't take a course on options and buy a calendar spread or credit spread. Don't do anything too complicated—do your analysis, find the right put, but **don't overthink**. Pfizer is going to drop $10 billion in revenue within a year or two after Lipitor goes generic. Maybe more. It does not have anything close to replacement products. Revenue and profits will plunge. Current valuations do not reflect this plunge and this is a company with a stock driven by earnings for more than a decade. The dividend is almost 7 percent and unsustainable once revenues and profits fall. End of story—buy a put.

Going with the Flow: Many, perhaps most **great trades on the short side occur when a falling stock is in a falling market segment**. The fall of the market segment either accelerates the fall in the stock or, at a minimum, eliminates any momentum that might occur within the segment and stall the slide of the target company. Pfizer is a great example. Its segment, Big Pharma, has been sliding steadily for several years (as measured by the PPH or Pharmaceutical HOLDRS, an exchange traded fund representing large pharmaceutical firms) and has provided no support for PFE whatsoever. Of course, there are many great positions in losing companies within a winning segment, a good example being Palm, a

---

The Simple Story of the Cheesecake Factory

Simple can mean very simple, truly simple, like almost dumb simple. In the fall of 2007 ChangeWave and third-party data began to show problems in the restaurant sector, but without giving specific names. So, who to short? I reviewed about 10 companies and quickly settled on the Cheesecake Factory. Using data I found on the Internet through Yahoo and the company's website, I discovered that for years, Cheesecake Factory grew rapidly with the highest revenue per square foot operation in the casual dining segment. And I knew from personal experience they were at the high end for many of their diners—the Applebee family splurging to take Grandma out on her birthday, the high school first date, the payday celebration. I also sensed CAKE made a lot of revenue and profit margin from their bar operations, drinks at the table, and relatively expensive desserts. Well, for customers still coming in, this would be the first thing cut out in a recession. For customers stretched thin by the recession, Grandma would have to go back to Applebee's—or enjoy a picnic with homemade food. Simple data, simple analysis—and an 84 percent gain in less than nine weeks.

victim of the success of the iPhone and the Blackberry, these products driving the smart phone makers Apple and RIMM to new highs.

Intersecting Segments: Many companies touch several segments that are interrelated with relative degrees of correlation and interdependency. And occasionally you get a company sitting at the intersection of several sliding segments. One example was Martha Stewart Omnimedia (MSO). This company sat at the intersection of homebuilding and consumer discretionary spending as well as traditional media (it has TV shows). Housing was getting hit and therefore new home furnishings; ChangeWave survey data showed consumer discretionary spending would not rebound for Christmas 2007; and revenues for TV outlets were shrinking according to industry data. I recommended shorting MSO through puts on January 3, 2008; on January 16 the position was up 137 percent and I closed it out, rolling it into a longer term position that did not work and was closed with a loss of 57 percent. The net gain was about 60 percent over a seven month period as one leg of the trade—TV ad spending—stabilized.

The Binary or Paired Trade: Most of us began and continue to invest in long positions. Analysis and investment in a long position can also reveal great short opportunities—what many call a paired trade—and **paired trades coming off longs we know well are a great place to begin prospecting new short positions**. If you like Apple because of the iPhone, look at shorting Palm or Motorola, losers in the high-end PDA market with the advent of the iPhone.

Another example is that of Illumina. I followed, on the long side, this fabulous company and watched it go from $10 to $90 (adjusted for splits). Illumina made (and still makes) the equipment used more and more in labs to do genetic research. Their success came not just from a growing market but growing market share—and that share was coming right out of the hide of another publicly held company, Affymetrix—and a quick look at Figure 4.3 shows how a great paired trade can work.

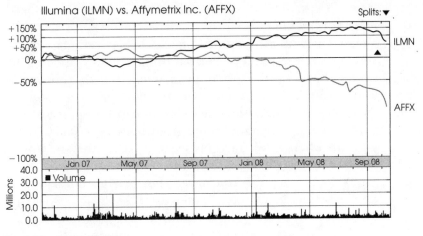

Figure 4.3   A Paired Trade

Source: CSI Data

From Prospecting to Analysis

The prospect's name is now on a list of potential shorts. Or in your head. Now it is time to look at some numbers, do some quick analysis. I emphasize the word quick. **There is no reason to get too fancy and draw angels on the head of a pin.** If something is not that obvious, move on; it is defying the rule of simplicity. Looking at the fundamental prospects of a company is the same whether you go long or short, buy equities or options. Choosing the right put does come into play—and the need for something to work in six months or less—and these differences drive some of the way you analyze an opportunity.

- **Time:** Think six months. Catalysts and/or Wall Street expectations need to change within six months, preferably sooner, to make a put position work. Yes, you can buy a LEAP almost two years out, but focusing on six months is best. A lot can change in two years and **your comfort zone for a trade should be no longer than six to seven months.** Does that mean you short a company, let's say Pfizer, only for a period of six months? No. Pfizer will be a potential short until it is $8 a share even if that takes three years. But it must start moving down within three months, six months at the outside, from the first time you buy a put on PFE if it is to be a viable position. The bottom line: Get yourself ahead of the fall.

- **Value:** The use of traditional metrics in a traditional way is a sure way to lose money when shorting. The only metrics that should concern you when prospecting for short positions are those that have prompted investors to go long a stock. If Starbucks stock has risen due to revenue growth per store, it is a potential short when revenue growth per store stalls. If Intel goes up when profit margins expand, short the stock when you think those profit margins will contract, and so on.

  What not to do? **You never short on traditional valuation alone**, even for overextended stocks. Strictly speaking, Microsoft was overvalued for more than a decade and broke the heart of many a short seller. The only metrics of value you need to worry about are those that analysts and others have used to drive up the price of the stock. If a stock has been rising due to top line revenue growth, and if profits hold up but top line growth surprisingly tails off, the stock is going to implode. For example, a cosmetic medical device company—lasers to remove tattoos and hair and other stuff—Palomar Medical (PMTI) rose from $6 to north of $52 in a couple of years due to solid profits but skyrocketing growth. Then, growth slowed and they missed top line estimates. In 15 months the stock lost 80 percent of its value even though profits fell less than half that percentage.

  The moral of this story? **Never, ever short on valuation alone**. Short based on what got them there.

- **Relative Value:** Relative valuation is another matter. This is the valuation the market is giving a stock compared to others in its market segment. Relative valuations often provide a floor or ceiling on stock prices. What do I mean by this?

  Every industry is measured and valued by analysts with standard metrics, most by price/earnings ratios. **Use a company's relative value to its industry when setting target prices for stocks**—a stock coming down may stabilize when its P/E, PEG ratio, or growth rate is at the industry average. This information is readily available on Yahoo—their industry centers within Personal Finance—and many other financial sites.

- **Decelerating Growth:** Growth is an attractive variable for many investors and the key for playing the short side is to measure whether growth is accelerating or decelerating. **And decelerating growth is a key feature of a potential short**. Some stocks may have climbed due to growth in their top line; some based on their bottom line; the stocks that appreciate the most in the shortest period of time, assuming sales and profits are driving valuations, are those with both accelerating revenue and profit growth. A company that grew 12 percent a year and is now growing 14 percent and has provided guidance it will grow 16 percent the next year is a Wall Street darling; a company that grows a steady 12 percent per annum for three years is a Wall Street favorite; a company that grew 12 percent last year, 10 percent this year, and will grow 8 percent next year is a great prospect for a short seller.

A great example of the impact of decelerating growth is the aforementioned Palomar Medical. This company was growing like weeds, 35 percent plus per annum for a while, with a high P/E. Then, one quarter, the company missed revenue growth by a wide margin and profits came in lower than expected but not off nearly as much as earnings. No matter. The stock had run based on revenue growth and fell 75 percent, from the low $40s to about $10 in a relatively short period of time when the Street no longer viewed Palomar as a growth company.

I like this metric—revenue growth—because it is simple, easy to calculate, and Wall Street likes it and uses it all the time.

- **Dividend Payouts:** Growing companies often pay solid dividends to share the wealth with shareholders and to increase the attractiveness of their stock. Failing companies offer very high dividends as a legal bribe to shareholders to hang onto the stock and not dump it, further depressing the price. Look for companies with too high dividend payouts—these perfectly legal bribes are typically unsustainable and when they get cut, BOOM, the stock takes a hit. For example, a sure sign of trouble at Fannie Mae was their unsustainable dividend and when they cut it to just a nickel, the stock went down 12 percent.

  How to determine if a dividend is too high? First, compare it to the average dividend in its industry segment. Second, if it is half again higher than the industry average— 50 percent higher—you have a warning sign or confirmation of a stock in trouble. This information is easily obtained at industry centers in the financial component of Yahoo.com and is also found at other financial sites.

Gauging Wall Street Expectations

Stock movements begin and end with Wall Street expectations—what analysts and professional investors think and expect. This pack of lemmings—excuse me, these professionals—drive institutional and much individual investing. So the short side investor needs to understand what their expectations are for a company and equity and what they consider to be good and bad news. This is both easier and harder than it looks.

Gauging Wall Street expectations can be tricky but false expectations can make you a lot of money. In 2007, many short-side traders made a boat load of profits on the home builders. There were several false bottoms put in underneath the sector—the slide in the stocks would stop, temporarily, and the pundits on CNBC and Fox Business would say they were now great values and a bottom or floor had been put in underneath these stocks. These foolish investors and pundits called five bottoms in 2007.

The Bankruptcy Short

The ultimate goal of a traditional short seller and even a put buyer is to see a company they are shorting to go bankrupt. There are companies that one can see as logical candidates for bankruptcy—Freddie Mac and Fannie Mae come to mind, and that story came true when Uncle Sam put them into receivership. Playing a short side trade to bankruptcy is hard to do, as bankruptcy becomes possible, premiums on puts expand greatly and the risk/reward profile of the trade becomes less and less favorable. I never recommended puts on Freddie or Fannie because of a fear of government intervention that would destroy the position. By the time I believed any intervention would wipe out shareholders, the premiums on the puts were saying many agreed with me and a buyer of these puts could not even get barely double in the event they went bankrupt.

In the fall 2006 I recommended opening what turned out to be a highly successful series of trades or rolled positions in Vonage. My recommendation was based on ChangeWave Research data that showed they would lose or stall out in adding subscribers, and public data that showed it lost money on every new customer it signed up—no kidding—a prescription for bankruptcy. It

(Continued)

produced gains of 43 percent, 175 percent, and 173 percent through careful management of new puts at new strike prices and expiration dates. And then I got too close to the end game—and put premiums were too high—and I took a hit on the last position, a loss of 67 percent. The total return on the position was 324 percent, much better than a traditional short position, but there was also a lesson learned. And Vonage is still around.

The lesson? The end game, the true bankruptcy short is more the province of professional investors borrowing shares in the hope they never have to be repaid.

There are various ways in which investors should gauge Wall Street's expectations.

Earnings

The simplest way to gauge Wall Street expectations is to look at consensus estimates for revenues and earnings for a particular company. This information is readily available in many places online. It is also important to gauge what are called "whisper estimates"—what traders on Wall Street are actually expecting and these are often different from consensus estimates. You may have to dig a bit and read articles and individual analyst reports to try to get a handle on these hidden expectations, and sometimes it is just not possible.

An equally important component in assessing earnings expectations is the industry leader—the bellwether company whose earnings can move other stocks in the industry. A great report from Intel will pull up all semiconductor stocks for a while; ditto for a discount retailer like Wal-Mart, or in the halcyon days of mortgages for everyone, any home builder. You need to be aware how a position can take a temporary hit due to a good earnings report from someone else in their segment.

Exogenous Data

Another way to gauge Wall Street's expectations is to look at exogenous data. This is such a large category I need to confine myself to what is most immediately useful—third-party data that move a stock, not just provide insight into a company's or segment's performance. What do I mean?

There are many third-party data services that make predictions from how many homes will be sold to how much fertilizer will be used on farms. This data move markets and stocks—and you need to be aware, at a minimum, of what data will move your position so you can time or better manage this position. For example, do you want to buy a put on a retailer the day before official numbers from the Department of Commerce? One way to check is to see what the forecast from that organization might be or what analysts on Wall Street are expecting. ChangeWave Research survey data is often ahead of other third-party data and when it is different from analyst expectations for a segment or a company it is like shooting the proverbial fish in a barrel. And data for a segment will often move all stocks in that segment.

For example, a company called IMS publishes monthly data on subscriptions. This is expensive data to buy, but leaks out through analyst comments and so on. If you short a Big Pharma or other drug company based on a belief that sales will slow, find a data source that quotes IMS data, leaks it, or otherwise gives you a look at the data as soon as possible.

Catalysts

You should also look at catalysts. A catalyst is what it sounds like—something that serves to change the opinion of investors about a company and therefore moves the stock. Some come out of nowhere; many are known to be on the horizon, such as earnings announcements. Catalysts reflect changes or continuation of trends in company fundamentals and the best thing for a short-side investor is to have a view of an upcoming catalyst that is both correct and contrarian to opinions on Wall Street.

Intrinsic

An intrinsic catalyst is something completely under the control of a company—an earnings announcement, a successful or unsuccessful sales launch, weak or strong monthly sales data, and so on. They vary by segment and company. For example, in cable and telecommunications the number of subscribers and the average revenue per subscriber is often more important than quarterly profit figures. The most important intrinsic catalysts are those tied most directly to the valuation metrics used by Wall Street to measure the worth of a company and establish the price of its stock.

For example, the cable industry in this country has, based on traditional views of profits and losses, never made a penny. The industry is measured by EBITDA (earnings before interest, taxes, depreciation, and amortization) and increasingly by free cash flow and the number of subscribers. In addition, subscriber growth, average revenue per subscriber, and the growth in that data point are used as predictive measures for EBITDA and cash flow. So monthly subscriber data have outsized impact on Wall Street's view of the near- and longer-term future performance of a cable company—and will move the stock accordingly based on these data.

There are many kinds of intrinsic catalysts other than financial or sales figures. They vary by stock, and by industry segment—and you can discover them by reading through company press releases and magazine articles and see how the company's stock moves in the immediate time period following this news or release of data.

Exogenous

External or exogenous data hit segments and individual stocks every hour of every day. The best approach for a professional or individual investor is to map out potential catalysts affecting a company or its industry segment based on history. Some are obvious. For example, for a biotech, an FDA approval date; for a home builder, the release of monthly new home sales data. Others less so—for example, monthly auto sales figures impact platinum mining stocks. Say what? Platinum is a critical and necessary ingredient in catalytic converters. Any map or list of potential catalysts for a segment or company will be incomplete—but putting one together is an excellent exercise that will contribute greatly to your selection of the correct strike price and date for a put on a company.

The Deadly Surprise

The deadly surprise is the fear of every investor, long or short. And when you hold puts, they can kill a position. Are they avoidable?

Yes and no—depends on your definition of surprise. An acquisition of a company totally out of the blue is something that just happens; the acquisition of a company that had been in play and then escaped an acquirer just three months before is not that much of a surprise. Look hard at what has been written and said about your target and then make your best judgment about potential deadly surprises—**and if you smell trouble of any sort, move on**. This caution has cost my subs some money as I have avoided stocks I felt could be helped out by a deadly surprise, but with my first rule being capital preservation, my second looking for a home run, my third you do both by waiting for the great trade—well, any doubts make it less than a great trade, so do not have regrets about moving on if you fear a deadly surprise.

One note about government created deadly surprises: You can, for the most part, avoid these. I stay away, and believe you should do the same, from companies where there is a probability Uncle Sam will come in and mess up a position. I never recommended shorting Freddie Mac or Fannie Mae for this reason; there are several dead biotechs being kept on life support by government contracts orchestrated by Congress protecting millionaires, excuse me, jobs in their home district.

Conclusion

You can do it. Repeat after me, you can do it. And remember, this is only the part where you are selecting the target based on fundamental weakness. In Chapter 5 you will look at a lot more stuff to determine if the technical stars are in alignment and you will actually create a position.

This part of the process—selecting the target based on fundamentals—is really the fun and intuitive part and I hope you use this chapter as a series of steps and guideposts that should be used with flexibility and creativity. I can explain a short position on Pfizer based on Lipitor in a nanosecond. Take out $10- to $12 billion in revenue beginning in 2011 or so and based on industry and historical valuations the stock is worth $8 bucks in two to three years. **That is the goal before you go to technical indicators—the elevator pitch, the simple explanation that everyone understands**. And then back that up with some light research. All of the steps I outlined above should not take more than an hour, depending on how rude your children are or how big your dog's bladder is, maybe two.

Q&A

Q1. Can I skip any of those steps? What are more important than others?

You can skip them all—it's your money. I am not suggesting a rigid formula—I have a method that works well for me and my subscribers, and I am suggesting you consider using it.

The most important steps are the first two: Keep a selection of a target simple and use common sense to vet that first selection. Why? Because you, and your instincts, work better than you know. And, when you want other investors to get in on your side, after you are already in, the simpler and therefore the more compelling the story the more investors will pile in when things go bad.

The other thing you have to do—and this you must do—is gauge Wall Street expectations. You gotta know why the stock price is where it is and what will bring it down or move it up. Spend a little time, spend more time, but you need to understand this in order to establish target prices and the actual put position.

Let me tell you a story about how to ignore this advice and lose money, from, ah, personal experience. It is actually a story about a long position—calls on Intel, lots of call options, too many—that I bought in anticipation that Intel would beat estimates. Published estimates. I was driving to a closing on the sale of a home in the country with my wife, it was after the market closed, and Intel's earnings were reported on the radio. I was ecstatic. They beat expectations. I started doing mental calculations and plans for spending and investing the profits. When I got back and checked the computer, those plans changed—the stock was down more than 5 percent in after-hours trading. I began reading and it turns out the whisper number for Intel was much, much higher than published estimates. Worse, a search of the Web shows I could have found this out if I looked. The next morning I sold off my calls, took the money, and spent what was left of the position on breakfast.

Q2. Can I really trust my intuition or my current process for selecting longs to develop a list of short prospects?

Yes to intuition, yes to instincts, yes to your process for selecting longs.

Intuition: This is another term for nonlinear but rational thinking. Malcolm Gladwell made millions explaining this in *Blink*. A great starting place.

Current process: Picking a target for the downside is the same as the upside. And, when you think just a little bit past picking a long, you

(Continued)

can always see a short on the horizon. If you go long on Apple due to iPhone sales, a falloff in sales by Palm and Motorola is right around the corner. If you go long on Bombardier because railroad car sales increased 40 percent, maybe it is time to short GM (actually, it is almost always time to short GM, the worst-managed company in America).

Q3. If the Fed raises interest rates, or they climb on their own, what does this do to high-dividend stocks?

They go down, almost reflexively. When you buy a high-dividend stock you look at the dividend compared to the interest on a Treasury bond. The difference between the two reflects the market's view of the risk in the stock—some would argue with the simplicity of this explanation but it suffices for now—and the higher the dividend the more the market is concerned with the stock declining or the dividend being cut, or both.

Q4. Can't I just trade based on charts, on momentum, and other indicators once bad news is out?

Sure—just don't tell anyone you read my book.

Rules

- The key to successful shorting any part of the market is sticking to fundamentals.
- When you pick a target company to short, act like an investor, not a trader.
- When you create, manage, and exit a position, act like a trader.
- Wait for the great trade to come to you.
- Great trades occur when a falling stock is in a falling market segment.
- Always go with common sense.
- Keep your story and position simple. Don't get fancy. Don't overthink.
- Paired trades coming off longs we know well are a great place to begin to prospect new short positions.
- Your comfort zone for a trade should be no longer than six to seven months.
- You never short on valuation alone.
- Use a company's relative value to its industry when you set target prices for stocks.
- Decelerating growth is a key feature of a potential short.
- Failing companies offer high dividends as a bribe to shareholders.
- The true bankruptcy short is more the province of professional investors who borrow shares in the hope they never have to be repaid.
- The simplest way to gauge Wall Street expectations is to look at consensus estimates.
- If you smell trouble of any sort, move on.

CHAPTER 5

Technical Indicators—You Gotta Love This Chart

I have yet to find a book or service that tries to instruct individuals on methods to short stocks that is not almost completely dependent on technical analysis and trading. I believe the best approach in selecting equities to short is based on fundamentals—a lousy company will eventually equate to a lousy stock, the kind of stock you make a great deal of profits from when playing the short side. That being said **you need to be mindful of some technical factors when buying and managing put positions**—because sometimes "eventually" can be too long to justify a put position. And this is what I want to briefly cover—how to use technical indicators to affirm or reject a potential short position. Why? Technical indicators are more important for puts than stocks and using them is like using other data you use to make stock selections.

This material is not sophisticated or comprehensive, but using technical indicators as I do when establishing short positions works very, very well. Just stick to some of the following basics and you will stay out of trouble—you will avoid shorting a lousy company with a strong stock.

Use technical indicators within your comfort zone; learn more about their value to your style of investing over time and ignore jargon and the gee-whiz aspect of technical information. It is valuable to technical traders and a distraction for you when building a put position to invest against a failing company.

One of my sons began investing when he was 13 and used basic Yahoo charts—he made a lot more money than most people (on a percentage basis) and still prefers to take his clues from the simplest of charts. And that is the key—just as with your fundamental analysis—**keep it simple when using not just charts but all technical indicators**. One big reason: Other investors are also keeping it simple and are using indicators to drive their investments. You need to be aware of what the crowd is doing so they don't run you over, and simple technical indicators are a great way to gauge the crowd.

If you feel you are a sophisticated technician move on to other chapters; this will bore you. Maybe.

Getting Started—Basic Charts

You gotta start somewhere—and the best places to begin working with technical indicators are basic charts that not only tell great technical stories—where a stock has been, where it might be going—they also reveal what other investors may be thinking, for they look at the same basic charts you do.

The basic chart is the chart you will find on most financial websites or in software used by online brokerages. The basic chart comes in many flavors such as five days, a month, three months, six months, a year, two years, five years, and so on. Figure 5.1 is

Figure 5.1   Pfizer Inc. as of 8/25/08

Source: CSI Data

the classic, basic one-year chart for Pfizer and gives you a good indication of what has transpired over 12 months without having to absorb too many numbers and other data points.

There are so many charts it is hard to identify what works best for what stock—and what works best for you. Everyone has their favorite—the 14-day stochastic, the one year parabolic, and so on.

As expected, I suggest that you keep it simple—if you currently use charts for creating positions, use the same ones when looking at short opportunities. If you do not use charts, do the following:

- Use charts to confirm a position you are prospecting, not to find one or to trigger a trade independent of fundamentals.
- Use basic charts to quickly plot out other technical indicators that support creating and setting target prices for your positions—later on I will discuss the importance of other technical indicators such as moving averages and money flows. Basic charts give you an excellent, instantaneous picture of the 50- and 200-day moving averages of a stock as well as the six-month and one-year lows. Basic charts can also show you money flows. Use these four charts as part of your initial look at technical indicators for a position.
- Use variations of these charts as often as possible. For example, the Pfizer chart displayed in Figure 5.1 is a stand-alone representation of the stock's movement for a year. But if you want to know, quickly, how Pfizer performed compared to its market segment, run Pfizer against the ETF for its segment, the PPH.
- Get a feel for the chart patterns—some of us are more visual than others—and over time build on the set of charts you feel most useful.

Complex charts are terrific tools for technical traders but an utter waste of time for what we are trying to do. Sorry, no super fancy stuff to brag about at the office.

More than Charts: Other Key Indicators

Charts are fast, easy-to-use, and drive other investors' behavior. But they are only part of the technical story driving a stock. There are other indicators that are critical to developing a winning short position. These indicators may relate to the movement of a stock such as a moving average or may relate directly to puts, such as the put/call ratio.

Moving Averages

Moving averages (MA) are important for short-side investing. I prefer the 50-day moving average for stocks and market segments, the 50-day and the 200-day moving average for indices—U.S. and foreign. These indicators can serve as a bottom, a ceiling, or parameters for the movement of a stock. If a stock has just broken above its 50-day moving average and stayed there for more than a couple of days, I will wait until it settles at or below that line before I buy a put. The same holds true for the 200-day MA and indices—I will wait until this technical indicator turns in my favor. (See Figure 5.2.)

The Put/Call Ratio

The put/call ratio is the measure that I find to be the simplest, fastest way to gauge changes in expectations for a stock. It is something you have to track each day. I have not found a service that tracks and plots changes in the put/call ratio in a simple fashion. You can guess what this measures—the number of puts outstanding divided by the number of calls outstanding. If this is increasing, negative

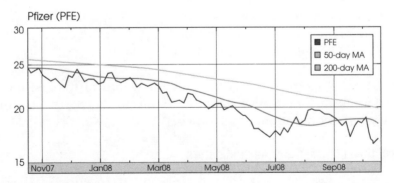

Figure 5.2   The Moving Averages

Source: CSI Data

sentiment is increasing. If it is decreasing, negative sentiment is decreasing.

When you use this measure, you should check it, if possible, against competitors or major players in a company's market segment. Often an entire segment will fall in or out of favor and this ratio will be explaining Street sentiment about the entire segment, not the individual stock in question.

Traders and momentum investors love this measure. You need to keep an eye on this, at a minimum, to see if you are entering a position running strongly with or against momentum on Wall Street. One other note: Check to see if this ratio differs greatly by month. Let's say there are an equal number of puts and calls outstanding in November and in December the number of puts outstanding is 30 percent greater than the number of calls. This means option traders are expecting bad things to happen to the stock.

One caveat, writing puts is an increasingly popular method for going long on a stock and in some cases may make the put/ call ratio seem too bearish. For example, you think a $50 stock will rise—instead of buying a $55 call, you sell a $45 put. No one is going to exercise a put in the money. That would mean the holder of the put, the person you sold it to, would have to go out and buy the stock at $55 and sell it to you at $45. The drawback in these positions is they tie up capital. Brokers typically require individual investors to hold enough funds in an account to buy the stock if it is put to them.

Shares Held Short

Check the number and percentage of the company's shares held short as often as possible. In theory the movement in the number of shares held short should parallel the put/call ratio but this often is not the case. Shorting shares is often the province of the slightly more patient trader or speculator than the put/call ratio. If you think a company is going to blow up by a specific date you buy the put closest to that date. The real metric you need to know is the change in the number of shares held short and the direction that number is going. Several services sell that information, organized on a daily basis. **If the number of shares held short is consistently shrinking, expectations are improving or a stock is seen to be nearing a bottom**; if the inverse is true, the Street sees more bad news ahead. The best short positions are contrarian, which means not many shares would be held short. Good rules of thumb are:

- You are truly ahead of the pack—an early short seller—when the number of shares held short is less than 5 percent of shares outstanding.
- You are gaining momentum in your position when 15 percent of shares are held outstanding.
- You need to be prepared for short-covering rallies when 25 percent of shares or more are held short.
- You are going to see manic volume days driven by short covering and potential short squeezes when 50 percent of shares or more are held short.
- When short shares are greater than 50 percent of shares outstanding—and I still recommend some positions, albeit not many, when this is true—you will see almost unreal reactions to news. Bad news will often drive prices up as shorts cover. I mention this because as an owner of puts, you need to be prepared for this level of volatility and temporary chaos when holding puts on an equity with a huge short position.

Days to Cover

Days to cover is another great indicator and is an early-warning sign of potential short covering rallies. The days to cover is a quick but highly useful measure of the potential impact of short covering—investors with short positions buying back shares—and a possible short squeeze, a dramatic rise in the price of a stock based on the buying back of shares by short side investors. This number tells us how long it would take for all shorts positioned to be covered by taking the number of shares held short and dividing it by average daily volume. If the number is low—say one or five or even 10 days to cover—volatility related to short covering will be low.

When you look at data on a stock and you see it takes more than 10 days to cover the outstanding short positions, consider it a warning. The volatility in the underlying stock could be greater than the market. This early warning signal is telling you the stock may be susceptible to short-covering rallies where investors shorting a stock buy back shares when news, good or bad, breaks about that company and stock.

A word of caution: Many heavily shorted stocks actually have relatively few days to cover because the average volume of trading in the stock is high due to, you guessed it, short selling and short covering. This amount of short selling and short covering distorts average trading volumes and makes this measure either meaningless or misleading. A variation of this is a rise or decline in the days to cover—clear signals of declining or increasing downside sentiment about the stock. If the days to cover is decreasing steadily, downside sentiment is waning; if days to cover is increasing, the inverse is true.

Volatility

Volatility is a term Wall Street loves to use rather than the simpler term "bouncing around." Technically, volatility of an individual stock reflects how much more, or less, it moves up, or down, compared to the market in general. The measure for the volatility of a stock is its beta, also an elegant term, and mysterious, too. The beta of a stock tells us how much it will trade with the market. A neutral beta means that on a typical day an equity moves on a percentage basis as much as the market does. A low beta means it moves less, a high beta means it moves more.

As put buyers, we (a) like high beta stocks if we have the stomach for managing highly volatile puts for they can produce larger returns faster; and we also like (b) low beta stocks because the premiums on puts of low beta stocks can be considerably less than on high beta stocks. Or so the theory goes. In reality, beta doesn't mean that much when creating positions based on fundamental weakness in the underlying company. But you should be aware of beta when making decisions about managing a position.

Liquidity

Liquidity is an important measure for us short sellers—illiquid put positions are not positions you want to enter. Liquidity refers to how many shares or option contracts are floating—able to be purchased—and how much trading in that equity or option contract occurs on average each day. For our purposes we are concerned with the liquidity in the put options—all the put options outstanding and the number of contracts trading at a specific price on a specific expiration date.

Based on trading trends in the last few years, you are definitely reading the right book: The trading of option contracts has exploded. According to data available on the Chicago Board Options Exchange (CBOE) there were 404,887 puts and calls traded on October 17, 2003, and 4,124, 680 puts and calls traded less than five years later on July 17, 2007, a tenfold increase. This shift to trading puts is reinforced by an explosion in short selling; since the lifting of the uptick rule in July 2007, short selling has exploded and more than $100 billion in equities have been sold short in the past 12 months, a huge increase.

The daily volume for a specific put position and the number of contracts outstanding are found on most financial websites. Daily volume is less important than the actual number of open contracts—that is the true measure of liquidity and investor interest in a specific position.

Money Flows

Money flows show how much investors are interested in a stock whether they want more of it or less of it. If more money is flowing into a stock—and steadily increasing or decreasing—it is an indicator, at a minimum, of interest in a company or an upcoming major event, such as an earnings announcement. A simple way to measure flows is to take the number of shares traded in a day, divide that into the number of shares traded on the Dow/Amex or NASDAQ, whichever is appropriate, and come up with a number. If that number is consistently rising, there is increasing interest in the stock and vice versa. (See Figure 5.3.) Here is what you do next.

What Was the Uptick Rule?

Most modern financial regulation in the United States began or was reinvented in response to the crash of 1929. During the crash and afterward a great deal of insider short selling occurred and, of course, this activity was assigned blame when people looked around for an explanation of the financial crisis. With the creation of the Securities and Exchange Commission in the 1930s came regulations to limit short selling. One such regulation became known as the Uptick Rule, which required all short sales to occur after an uptick in the stock price. This regulation went the way of the dinosaur in July 2007 and two consequences have been a marked increase in volatility and a large increase in the number of shares actively being shorted in the first year the markets operated without the Uptick Rule.

Money Flows

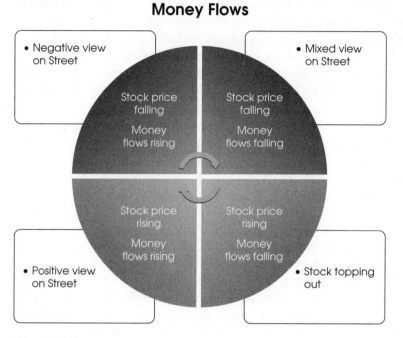

Figure 5.3   Money Flows

- If the stock price is falling while money flows are increasing, it is a great sign that expectations are not good at all.
- If the stock price is falling and money flows are decreasing, there is a lack of buyers, the Street is losing interest in the company's story, but there are still not as many active sellers as there might be—views of the stock on the Street are mixed.
- If the stock price is rising while money flows are increasing, this is a great sign the Street thinks good things are about to happen.
- If the stock price is rising and money flows are decreasing, it means the stock is probably nearing the higher end of expectations and could be on the verge of topping out.

Do this for the relevant market segment as well—sometimes interest in a segment can completely skew money flows into an individual stock.

Bottom line: **Heavy money flows with an upward bias into a stock or segment can hurt a short position. Do not buy a put when this is happening and if the stock is trading with the segment**.

I learned about the importance of money flows the hard way. My subscribers did well—very well—when I recommended shorting Amgen. Actually, they made money with Amgen from $55 down to near $40. I felt the stock was worth no more than $30 to $35 due to a big falloff in sales of their core anemia drugs. I was right and wrong. I was right about the fundamentals—sales took a big hit, earnings were flat, and I expected the stock to move down further. The stock bounced back to above $60. Why? Money flows—in a volatile and uncertain market—were heading to all big cap, cash rich biotechs such as Amgen, as evidenced by flow into the BBH, the equivalent of an ETF on biotech. The entire sector outperformed the market by more than 25 percent over a nine-month period, and while Amgen had a weakening present and a bleaker future, it was still profitable, free of debt, and loaded with cash. Never again—**you should check money flows religiously before opening a position.** Money flows are shown at the bottom of Figure 5.4—the series of peaks and valleys, peaks being more money going into a stock, valleys, less.

One issue with using money flows as an indicator is that short-term traders will hijack a stock or market segment when it gets hot—going up or down—and it is almost impossible to know how

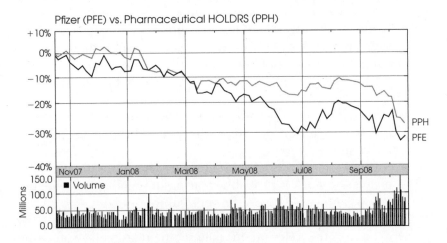

Figure 5.4   Performance Against Market Segment

Source: CSI Data

much of the money coming in is from longer term investors who will support the stock price and traders.

Previous Lows and Highs

Previous lows and highs are an easy tool to use when establishing a position and targets for that position. I am a simple guy, and not only do I really like using simple moving averages, **I really like using previous highs and lows to provide a box around where I think a stock can go**. A simple chart will show you a previous low—and shockingly you will see how, over and over again, stocks and ETFs and indices hit previous lows and highs and often bounce off them like a yo-yo, if only temporarily. I set target prices for stocks—not puts—and that target price is invariably linked to a previous low or, if I am waiting for a stock or index to take a turn, a previous high.

You need to frame these highs and lows. For stocks and ETFs I almost always look at six months, occasionally longer if something jumps off the chart. For indices such as the S&P **I look at all three simple charts—90 day, 180 day, and one-year performance**.

Conclusion

I love fundamentals, but I also know, and you need to know, you cannot establish successful put positions unless technical indicators are flashing green. People look at technical indicators to ascertain momentum in a stock and that in turn is used to not just determine if a trade will work but at what entry points and when. Technical indicators are also useful in setting target prices (I will get to that soon), but assistance in creating the when—the timing of the creation of the position—is the paramount value of technical indicators.

You cannot time the market or time an individual equity. You can either get ahead of a big movement and manage a position that may work against you for a while, or you can get into a position once it starts to move in the correct direction. This is true for long and short positions. It is important when buying and managing put positions— if you get too far ahead of a downward move, you can be 50 percent, or more, under water before that position turns into something hard to manage and a move that also reduces your potential profit.

Also, I believe you should not fight technical indicators. The example of Pfizer comes to mind. I watched it go from $28 to $20 but trading in the stock did not provide a clear technical direction. I then piled on at \$20 because I had a great deal of certainty, technically, that the stock was going to move sharply to the downside in a relatively short period of time. I made less money but put less at risk.

And, due to this belief, **I would err on the side of jumping on a position later rather than sooner.** Give up a little bit of your profit to protect a big share of your investment capital.

Q&A

Q1. If there is a large short position in a stock, should you avoid shorting it?

Not necessarily. It depends on your time horizon, the average trading volume, and your ability to manage through upticks in the stock caused by short covering. If there is a large short position in a stock but the average daily trading volume is high, then the days to cover may be small and short-covering rallies may not hit you too hard. Also, you may have a long-term time horizon—at least two months or more—and you know the stock will settle into a downward trend after a short-covering rally. If you plan to exit the position soon I would avoid puts that could go against you due to short covering.

Q2. How do I measure flows into a stock and a segment?

For a stock, look at the average daily trading volume and also look at a two-year chart that has volume—Yahoo has this; most charts do—so you can see if volume is seasonal. Then compare this movement to the market in general. For a segment, you can see it by looking at the indicators for an ETF, preferably the largest ETF for a segment.

Q3. I was looking at a put position and it seemed like the number of puts outstanding was five times the number of calls—the close in puts that expired within 90 days. What is that telling me?

Sometimes a lot, sometimes a little.

Most of the time this means traders think something bad is going to be announced within 90 days—it can be as simple as that. Sometimes it is fund managers thinking the stock will go up, although it is rare that you hear of a large volume of puts being sold as part of long strategy.

Q4. When the market has a down day and my stocks are hit hard I feel I am at risk. Explain again why volatility and risk are different?

If you look at your accounts every day as if you need the money that day (and you do need the money that day), then volatility is risk.

(Continued)

Other than that, volatility is the movement of a stock or option or whatever, up or down, and it is an independent variable when looking at the fundamental soundness of your position. Citigroup's stock bouncing around does not mean any fundamentals have changed or that there is inherent risk in the put position.

I would like to add two caveats: If the volatility of a stock increases after you buy a put and that volatility is matched by the volatility in the put, then the premium may expand as the perceived risk in the stock and the put increase. The other caveat is time: If you have a put near expiration that is volatile, timing your exit can be difficult and you may have to sell early to avoid a downdraft in the value of the put just before expiration.

Rules

- You need to be mindful of some technical factors when buying and managing put positions.
- Use technical indicators within your comfort zone.
- Keep it simple when using all technical indicators, including charts.
- Use charts to confirm a position you are prospecting, not to find one or to trigger a trade independent of fundamentals.
- Use basic charts to quickly plot out the technical indicators that support creating and setting target prices for your positions.
- Moving averages are important for short-side investing.
- The put/call ratio is the measure that I find to be the simplest, fastest way to gauge changes in expectations for a stock.
- Check the number and percentage of a company's shares held short as often as possible.
- Days to cover is another great indicator and is an early-warning sign of potential short-covering rallies.
- If the number of shares held short is consistently shrinking, expectations are improving or a stock is seen to be nearing a bottom.
- Heavy money flows with an upward bias into a stock or segment can hurt a short position. Do not buy a put when this is happening and if the stock is trading with the segment.
- Use previous highs and lows to provide a box around where you think a stock can go.
- You cannot time the market or time an individual equity.
- Do not fight technical indicators.
- Err on the side of jumping on a position later rather than sooner.

Creating a Position

If this book were a magazine article, it would be this chapter, for what you have read is pulled together here—and when you go through this material you may want to take a look at a couple of your favorite dogs and walk through these steps to analyze those potential positions.

Grab your coffee: here we go.

Getting Started

There are a few steps that you must do when you create a short position.

1. **Select What Capital to Use:** You need to determine what account and what part of your portfolio will be used to fund a position. As I wrote before, this should initially be the higher risk component of your portfolio. Assuming you are going to be shorting stocks for a while, and using puts as suggested, you should allocate no more than 5 percent of your high risk capital, preferably less, to your first trade or to a typical trade.

2. **Select a Specific Account:** A trading account is the natural place for this activity. If you opt to do this in a retirement account and your broker says he or she cannot let you buy options in a retirement account, get a new broker. This is to avoid a nasty situation—you get margin calls and your broker sells other positions to meet margin calls. No sane broker will let you short stocks in a retirement account.

3. **Determine the Entry Point:** Puts move fast—you have selected a put based on a certain price of the stock and the put. If the market is calm and the stock is trading the same way, put in a limit order for the entire lot of contracts you want and wait it out. If the stock is moving fast, put in your order for a put, see what happens for 15 to 30 minutes, and if it does not go off, raise your bid a bit—somewhere between a penny and a nickel. Different online brokerage houses have different capabilities for building positions and your ability to chase or wait in part depends on what they allow you to do.

   If that does not work, you have the following choices:
   - Determine how high can you can go and **put in a new limit order.**
   - **Look at a different put,** typically the next strike price.
   - **Wait it out**—leave a good until cancelled order for the day and go get some coffee. If that does not work, try again tomorrow.

   The key here is not to chase, and if the potential of the trade says to chase a bit, do it in a measured way. You can average up—but I don't believe in averaging down; it means you are putting more money in a position that is already a loser.

4. **Determine Target Prices:** You already have a target price for the stock. Your target price for a put should be a double/100 percent gain or whatever you are comfortable with. This does not mean you should hang on to any position until you get a double or hit a target you use for other option plays. You need to readjust your thinking as time passes, the stock and the put prices move. As Mike Tyson reminds us, everyone has a plan until they get punched in the mouth. Markets have a tendency to punch us all in the mouth now and again. Target prices should be changed over time.

5. **Determine When to Buy:** I have eyed positions for months before buying. Yes, I left money on the table but I was waiting for the low-risk great trade. The best example of this is a trade you could have made in Pfizer between mid-2007 and early 2008. The stock went from $28 to $20—slowly and steadily—but when it stayed below $20 for a few days, it broke and made a straight run to $16 and change. The best position would have been a short term option to play the quick break and a long-term put option called a LEAP to play the deteriorating

fundamentals in the company. This fundamental weakness was always there, but this is the most widely held stock in the United States, almost a cult stock, and until certain technical indicators flashed green, it was not yet time to go into a put position. When the stock broke, the signal would have been clear—time to get in.

Some simple rules to follow—first, **don't be the first one in**—don't be so far ahead of technical indicators you end up 50 percent under water before the position heads in your direction. Second, **never average down**—I said that before but it is worth saying it again—averaging down means you misread your entry point. This may mean you misread the entire position. Don't jump into a position telling yourself you can average down if you jumped in too soon.

6. **Set Time Stops:** You need to set a time stop, a date you tell yourself you will exit the position if it is at or below a certain price and before expiration. This is the voice of experience speaking. The 50 percent I got my subs in 2007 on the typical position would be higher if I had done this, and the 55 percent they saw in 2008 would be much higher if I had used time stops. I had read about time stops but did not use them as I thought they would work counter to my home run strategy—they do not. That being said, **do not make time stops an automatic trigger for a sale on all positions**, but you need this as a guide for managing some of the day-to-day fluctuations in the put price.

   There are several criteria for setting time stops. First, in an earnings-driven stock, you should set a time stop before or after the company announces earnings. You set the time stop before if the Street sees disappointing news ahead and there is considerable movement in the put. If you think earnings will truly surprise on the downside—remember those whisper numbers—your time stop is after the earnings announcement. In other stocks there are other catalysts; even in earnings-driven stocks there may be a strong catalyst that moves the stock. Use this to develop the date for the time stop.

   The bottom line: **the time stop is a self-imposed inflection point** to force you to step back and reevaluate the position asking the simple question: Would I buy that put now? If the answer is no, close the position.

A Company Not a Stock

Truly, if you get anything out of this book, you need to understand the importance of shorting companies and not stocks. Stocks move up, they move down, they can break your heart—short term. Longer term, they track the performance of companies. Always. Well, almost always.

Individual investors need to stick to fundamentals simply because they are individuals; investing and trading is not a full-time job. Even most money managers—more than 90 percent according to recent surveys—do not trade, they invest. So, aside from professional traders who work every day in front of their screens or have technical trading strategies that can be put in place in an automated fashion, individuals do best when sticking to fundamentals. Let the traders make their money on day or swing trades—you can make more money shorting lousy companies that ultimately destroy the value of their stocks.

You start with the story. Their story. Then you have your story, probably a contrarian story. Then you make lots of money when you are proven right.

Their Story

Most companies have a story—they may call it a strategy or plan— about where they are going and how they will perform in the current year. Even companies that do not provide financial guidance, such as Google, still present a view of the world and how they are going to conquer it, to investors. **The simplest way to identify an opportunity is to find a disconnect between the company story and your view of reality.**

Let's work with one example, Pfizer, a great company that is and will be stuck in deep yogurt for several years barring a major acquisition or stroke of incredible fortune in their laboratory. The entire world knows the patent on Lipitor is expiring in 2010 and it will face generic competition in 2010 or 2011. Although Lipitor is the world's leading drug with $12 to $13 billion in sales, it is losing share to generic statins such as Zocor. History and ChangeWave survey data tells us it is very probable 75 percent to 85 percent of this share will go away, 12 to 18 months after generics hit the market. The company story is this: Pfizer's pipeline and tight financial management will make up the difference in sales and profits. The reality: Its pipeline stinks, it has only begun to make cuts and it is selling the story along with a 6.5 percent to 7 percent dividend.

Wall Street's View

Wall Street expectations are split into two categories: published expectations, both quantitative (sales and earnings) and opinions (whether a drug will get approved or a product will succeed in the marketplace); and the hidden or whisper expectations, what traders are making bets on.

It is relatively easy to find published estimates and opinions. It is the whisper numbers that can give you a real headache after earnings are announced or after a press conference about a new product, and so on. The key to a successful short position is to ignore the whisper number and focus on the majority, well-known Wall Street opinion of a company. This set of expectations drives longer-term performance of a stock.

Sticking to the example of Pfizer, Wall Street still believes PFE can manage through the Lipitor expiration and maintain profits. Absurd, but there it is—overly optimistic expectations creating a great short position. As this goes to press, Pfizer has announced plans to acquire Wyeth. While M&A activity often hurts short positions, this proposed transaction reinforces the strength of this trade and the power of this example. The acquisition of Wyeth will not mitigate in a meaningful

Beware the Cult Story Stock

There are such things as cult companies and stocks. They are often called "story stocks" but their story is long over, and discovering you have bought a put on a cult stock can prove to be an expensive lesson learned. These cult companies are typically former market leaders still hanging around, perhaps even still chugging along, but truly failing. They may also be the makers of a ubiquitous or formerly popular product that prompts investors to say "they will figure it out." For example, almost everyone knows Palm and knows or knew someone who owned a Palm. And the company has been flailing and failing for a long time. If and when you find a company, prospect it, analyze, and go to create a position, be mindful of how long it has been a lousy company and how long it has lingered at a certain price point. If a company has been failing for more than 6 to 8 quarters, has a big brand name, yet the stock is flat, and has not reacted to bad news, you may want to walk away for it is obvious its cult status is keeping the stock afloat. **Cult stocks like Palm and Sun Microsystems can exist on air for years because they have cash and a history even if their market share shrinks and their prospects dim.**

way the loss of the Lipitor patent and will simply mask for a brief period of time the loss of revenues and profits at Pfizer. The addition of Wyeth revenues, if the deal goes through, will be more than offset by the dilution suffered by existing Pfizer shareholders, the loss of cash and increase in interest costs on new debt, and the inevitable reduction in the company's dividend. As you read through this example, you can see how the Lipitor story is so compelling the justification for the position does not change with the Wyeth deal. Financing is still uncertain, but please follow this example even if this is a reality as you read on—and contact me via e-mail, at mshulman@investormedia.com, if you want my current opinion of Pfizer.

The successful short investor looking at PFE sees a potential $10 billion hole in the company's revenue stream beginning in 2010/2011 that cannot be filled. This can be done as there are many articles showing how poor the company pipeline is at this time. That same investor's 14-year-old son looks at the P/E, does a simple calculation on where profits will be once that patent expires, and comes up with a stock price of $8 to $10. That same investor's mother, a more sophisticated type, sees a huge dividend totally out of proportion to historical trend and the rest of the industry—and industry worldwide to boot. Common sense says the dividend cannot survive once cost-cutting comes into play. Employees will not tolerate this bias toward shareholders. And the dividend will be less valuable when interest rates eventually rise.

My contrarian story? Lipitor is irreplaceable. End of story.

Data from a myriad number of patent expirations and generic drug introductions is as far as you need to go; from Claritin to Zocor the evidence shows a dramatic drop off in revenue in a very short period of time. Zocor is a direct competitor to Lipitor, and data on generic and branded Zocor sales, plus data from a third party source, in this case ChangeWave Research surveys, show sales will plummet—as much as 85 percent, perhaps as little as 60 percent—but we are still talking a giant revenue hole. To replace that Pfizer would have to introduce 10 new blockbusters in the next two years. There is a better chance my sons will take out the trash unprompted. End of story.

The Selection Process—Overview

Lotta stuff so far—let's put it all together with a look at the fundamentals of that one company—Pfizer. And to prove to you this is a simple exercise, everything shown below, except some ChangeWave Research survey data, you can find via the Yahoo! Personal Finance site.

Is it a potentially great, great trade? Yes—Pfizer is a hugely liquid stock with a large following, lots of puts outstanding, and the creator of the best-selling drug, right now and in the history of the world— the statin Lipitor. It is also a very fine company that thought it had a replacement for Lipitor, but it failed in trial. For purposes of full disclosure, I take Lipitor and most of the physicians I know personally take the drug prophylactically—it is that good a drug. And, as you will see, it is the ultimate simple, commonsense great trade.

No, someone from Pfizer did not run over my dog. I know several senior executives with the company and they are fine men and women—and no Big Pharma firm can match its standards for ethical behavior and even for being frank with shareholders. That said, it has a potential $10 billion hole in its future that is not negotiable— this is not my opinion. I am not recommending you go out and buy puts when you read this—publishers need time to bring books to market—but as I write this, PFE is an $8 stock posing as a $15 to $20 stock.

And, most on Wall Street think the company will "figure it out"— music to any short investor's ears—so this is a contrarian play as well. So let's walk through it.

- **Does it make sense?** Lipitor accounts for $12 to $13 billion in sales—25 percent of sales, maybe double that of profits. Take most of that away and *boom*, end of an era. Don't overthink it—generic Zocor whacked branded Zocor, generic Zocor is hurting Lipitor, generic Lipitor will kick, well, whatever, there might be some prodigies reading this.
- **Can I establish a simple position to make it work?** Liquidity makes this one of the easiest stocks around to short. Data on Lipitor sales is available monthly, the dates for the market entry of generic Lipitor are a bit murky but within a 12-month window ending in late 2011 all the information you need is public information.

Framing the Analysis

Next, you ask yourself four questions that will frame the analysis.

1. **Can this work in six months?** Even though this is a play on a change in their fortunes in 2011, the answer is yes. Analysts know what you know, they are just being much slower to react. The stock has fallen steadily, with bumps, from $28 to $20 and has not stayed at one level for more than a few weeks. (In my own service I recommended puts to $20, the stock fell to $16, I closed the shorter term position and kept open the 2010 LEAPS). The stock is on a temporary upturn and set up for a good entry point for an investor to buy a put.

2. **What is the value of the stock—and how is it measured?** PFE is a P/E driven stock—analysts have given up on growth—with a low P/E compared to its historical norm. Typically, PFE and other Big Pharma firms also include a certain amount of value in their stock prices based on their drugs in development but PFE has a weak pipeline that certainly cannot come close to replacing lost sales of Lipitor. You don't have to crunch many numbers—you can reduce profits 25 percent, the falloff in sales, or 50 percent—and you still get a great short position.

3. **What is the relative value of the stock?** The P/E and other measures of valuation are not out of line with other Big Pharma outfits. As I write this, it is just below 15, the industry's is just above. The company's product pipeline is quite weak compared to the size of the upcoming hit it will take from generic Lipitor.

4. **Are the dividend payouts low or high?** The dividend you see is very high—6.5 percent. What is the dividend payout of competitors? The average dividend for seven Big Pharma competitors is 2.95 percent. PFE is paying people to stay in its stock—not a bad thing if you are growing but if you are shrinking, that money would best be used elsewhere.

Also of note: Pfizer increased its dividend 10 percent in Q1 of 2008 as business and earnings were stagnant. Another bad sign the company is using its dividend to attract share holders.

Gauging Expectations

Pfizer is not only the most widely held stock in America, it is also one of the most widely covered with more than 30 analysts having opinions about the stock. In order to gauge your expectations, ask yourself:

- **What do earnings look like?** Consensus estimates for PFE, which you could find on Yahoo! Finance or any one of a number of websites, are for $2.37 in the current year—the stock is $20 a share—and $2.52 for the next fiscal year. How does an individual gauge whether these are appropriate, optimistic, or pessimistic? Go to the search function and type in "inflation in prescription drugs" and you see inflation in the cost of drugs is more than the 6 percent gain in earnings, which means PFE's earnings growth is based on price increases, not increased market share.

- **Is money flowing in or out?** There are a zillion ways to analyze this so remember, keep it simple. The simplest way is to look at a chart of money flows and compare it to a chart of the stock market in general—in this case, either the S&P or the Dow—and gauge it visually. Or, if you have a hyperactive math nerd hanging around the house, take the last 30 or 45 days of volume, divide that into the volume for the Dow, and see if the percentage is increasing, decreasing, or staying the same. In this case, volume tailed off as the price of the stock went up, and in the past 30 days or so volume is lighter than the rest of the Dow and S&P 500 as the price of the stock has risen.

- **How many shares are held short?** A meaningless amount— 1 percent of the float—which means PFE is an easy stock to short. The days to cover is actually more important, and is much more telling. That number tells us how long it would take for all short positions to be covered by taking the number of shares held short and dividing it by average daily volume. For PFE, it would take only 1.3 days of average volume to equal the number of shares held short—and this means that if shorts go to cover this position it will have only a minor impact on the stock price.

- **What does the put/call ratio look like?** Again, it serves to compare the put/call ratio to the world in general. You can go to Yahoo and find the PFE put/call ratio by doing some simple division. Check the ETF for Big Pharma—the PPH— and then check some other Big Pharma stocks. If you want to wander and get more confirmation, you can then look at that ratio compared to the current market, which is available at the Chicago Board Options Exchange. This will give you a sense of what Wall Street is thinking—if the number of puts to calls is increasing in Pfizer faster than it is in the general market, then negative sentiment is increasing at a faster rate than the markets in general. In this case, the put/call ratio for PFE is actually declining relative to the market—a great sign that sentiment about PFE is improving, setting up an even better short position.

- **What about exogenous data?** There is plenty of data about drugs, generic drugs, insurance reimbursement, and so on. You can find a good deal of this is free and accessible through a Yahoo or Google search. Wall Street has access to a good deal of proprietary data not generally available to the general public—including data from ChangeWave that I share with subscribers—and in this case, ignore it. Why? Go back to simplicity and common sense. Lipitor comes off patent, revenues crash, earnings decline, end of story. No data can change this.

    Whoa, Shulman. What if Pfizer does something, like, uh . . . ?

    What, cut prices? Same impact.

    I mean, how do you know. . . .

    Claritin lost more than 75 percent market share in a heartbeat. Branded Zocor, a direct competitor to Lipitor, lost gigantic amounts of share, and common sense—please, use common sense—says patients and payors prefer a $20 product to an $80 product.

Catalysts

Catalysts move stocks up or down. Potential, predictable catalysts for PFE are easy to find, and so are some of their dates. And remember, the true direction of a company will be based on fundamentals but catalysts move stocks. This is of critical importance when managing a shorter term—one- to six-month—put position.

- **Intrinsic catalysts:** Earnings, earnings, earnings. It's the earnings, stupid—earnings, not revenue growth, are the key to the PFE stock price. Dates for earnings announcements can be found on company websites and many financial websites so you know when news will break. Other intrinsic catalysts for PFE include Analyst Days or meetings—these dates are also publicly available—and they are opportunities for the company to impress or disappoint analysts.

- **Exogenous catalysts:** For a company in health care requiring FDA approvals and getting lots of dough from Medicare, most exogenous catalysts are related to the government. Companies publish timelines for clinical trials and drug approvals (or rejections) as does the FDA. In the case of PFE, there are no major FDA judgments looming—there are plenty of small ones—and the big potential government action is Medicare Part D. And here things get interesting, and again, it goes back to common sense. President Obama has made clear, given pressure on the budget and with a Democratic Congress, that it is logical to assume Medicare will get the right to negotiate drug prices sometime between mid- to the end of 2009.

  This is a big-time negative catalyst for the stock independent of the actual impact on revenue. The potential for this change needs to be factored into the target price set for PFE stock and the expiration date of the put used to create a short position.

- **Deadly surprises:** How do you predict the unpredictable for a company like PFE? You need to read. And what you will find is the company desperately needs to boost its new product pipelines, but at the same time the CEO has stated several times it does not intend to buy another Big Pharma or biotech company and is limiting potential acquisitions to the small, perhaps under $4 billion range. This statement and the company's needs mean the biggest logical deadly surprise would be an acquisition that would be a blockbuster and boost the stock price.

  So, what are the odds of this happening? Be arbitrary, be logical, have some fun—by this time you know more about the company without any previous biases than most of the lemmings on Wall Street. Let's say Pfizer will buy products, so there is a 100 percent chance they will acquire some companies. But smallish companies cannot help a $50 billion sales behemoth. So what are the odds the CEO changes his mind? Let's say 50 percent—that there is a 50/50 chance it makes a big blockbuster acquisition.

  What to do now? Spend 10 minutes, no more, have some coffee or something strong and think it through. What would a blockbuster acquisition have to look like? C'mon, put on your expert hat, have some fun.

- Product pipeline——Gotta change the product pipeline—strong products.
- Revenue growth—should be growing at least 20 percent a year, okay, maybe 15 percent. But they are not going to buy a slow grower, and if they did it will only reinforce a negative view of the company.
- Dilution—this is an earnings-driven stock. The acquisition needs to be what is called neutral or accretive. It cannot cause a drop in earnings per share. How does this happen? First, the company has to be as profitable as Pfizer. Second, Pfizer has to use a lot of cash to buy the company. If they use a lot of cash, they either use their own plus debt or use a mix of cash and stock. If they use too much cash, they will cut their dividend, a big prop for the stock. If they use too much debt, earnings will fall as they pay interest on the debt. Again, EPS can take a hit.
- Speaking of dilutive—the target is going to sell at a multiple at least twice that of PFE's—at least 30 times earnings. Current big cap biotechs sell in the low 20s and if you add a premium you get 30.
- So, with this being the P/E of the target, assume PFE would pay half cash, half stock, or all stock. Either way PFE will have to cut the dividend considerably.

Where does this leave you? Laughing at your worries, for only one company in the world fits this profile at the time you do this analysis. Those are long odds against an acquisition. And, if PFE did make this kind of purchase the stock would bounce up and your position would get whacked. Temporarily, then, analysts would crunch some numbers and the stock would, over time, retreat to a level determined by projected earnings.

What about someone acquiring PFE? Not with its market cap—way, way too big—end of story.

I know you won't do this kind of thinking, but it sure helps chill you out when worrying about a deadly surprise. So if you are afraid of the deadly surprise, take a half hour before creating a position and run yourself through this kind of process.

Be mindful of deadly surprises. Always. Looking at shorting oil? What is the probability the Israelis bomb Iran? Want to short Sun Microsystems? What is the possibility some Chinese company loses its mind and buys the company for its marquee value and installed base? Want to short Applebee's, what can help the restaurant chain that you cannot think of—oops, that happened, IHOP bought them. So, deadly surprises can happen.

Setting Price Targets

Time to get down to it: Let's say the stock is $20, has traded as low as $17. **The price is the driving factor in selecting the right put.**

Setting the target price for PFE is straightforward. You know they are going to have a big hole in their revenues in the coming years, you know the Street is steadily incorporating this into their estimates for revenue and profits, you know the stock is driven by profits, you know as the crunch hits the dividend will be cut, and you can guess they will cut back on some spending. Put this all together on the back of a napkin and then say what the hell, Lipitor is 25 percent of sales, let me run two numbers. A 25 percent cut in profits—the stock is $15—and a 50 percent drop in profits since Lipitor, according to what I have read, contributes a lot to profits. Now the stock is $10, or worse since one analyst suggested Lipitor is actually 65 percent of profits. The range for the fair price of the stock—assuming Wall Street prices in forward earnings 18 to 24 months before they hit—will be $8 to $10 sometime in 2010. The stock will bounce a bit, up and down, but should get there.

Technical Indicators
For Pfizer the technical indicators are simple to read.

- **Moving Averages:** You check to see if the stock has broken down, if it has busted through the 200- and 50-day moving averages, the 50-day MA being my favorite. It has and you now have a very good technical indicator that gives you a last green light to go ahead with a put position. But you should check other indicators.
- **Liquidity:** This is a nonissue for the most widely held stock in America.

- **Money Flows:** Check to see if money is flowing in and compare that to money flows into the ETF for the Big Pharma segment, the PPH. Let's assume there is no heavy money flowing into the stock.
- **Put/Call Ratio:** You are not able to measure trends but a quick check will tell you if it is a bullish or bearish indicator. Let's assume it is bearish. Another good sign.

Time to look at what put to buy.

Selecting the Right Put

Talk to yourself and tell yourself the following things matter.

- **I want leverage**—I want a home run if I believe this is a great idea. And to hit a home run I need some leverage.
- **I want a home run** because I am making a high risk investment.
- **I also want to play some defense**—I want to give myself some time in case the position moves against me for a period of time. This translates into a relatively lower priced (per contract) put with an expiration at least six months out.

  Okay, go to Yahoo or your brokerage site or DTN or wherever you get option quotes and do the following:
- **Play defense** and look at least six months out at puts. It is August so let's look at March puts.
- **Check to see what is available** and you find a put buyers' dream. The $20 puts are trading at $1.78 with the stock trading at $19.88. That is $1.66 time value for the put over seven months—a low time value and that makes the premium on the put low—downright cheap given your view of the company.
- **You take a position** equal to 2.5 percent of your high-risk capital.

Conclusion

All of this analysis in thinking does not take long or involve any expertise in drugs, manipulating the Internet, or financial analysis. Why? Because it is a great idea, a simple idea, and it makes common sense.

My conclusion? You can do it. Sounds too simple? Think of these other examples.

Microsoft introduces Vista to overwhelmingly negative reviews. Well, that means buyers may look to alternatives, and the only one is Apple. Does that make Microsoft a short? No, but you discover Apple at $36 and sell it at $184. Just simple, common sense.

Fannie Mae had more than $2.5 trillion in bonds outstanding supported by $50 billion in what the government says is equity and less than $20 billion in what Wall Street considers to be equity. That means it was leveraged 125 to one—and it means if less than 1 percent of loans default in the worst housing crisis since the depression its equity is wiped out. Common sense prevails, the stock falls more than 90 percent in a year, and eventually Uncle Sam takes over.

My point? You can do it.

Q&A

Q1. I find it hard to believe Wall Street is that lame—that they don't see the weakness in Pfizer that you say we can see.

A good point, but remember, not everyone sat in the front of the classroom, and let me ask you to review the chart I showed above on Schering Plough. This company, the maker of Claritin, took many quarters to slide although everyone knew when the patent for Claritin expired and what was going to happen to sales—or should have known, except for the many professional investors who thought they would figure it out.

Embrace Wall Street's collective stupidity—it will make you a lot of dough.

Still don't believe me? Before 2008 Bill Miller was one of the most successful mutual fund managers around consistently outperforming the S&P. He called a bottom in financial stocks and by mid-2008 had loaded up on Fannie and Freddie, ending up being Fannie Mae's largest shareholder. He just looked at charts, old patterns, and book values that drove both—and ignored that book values were ephemeral due to what these values were based on—toxic waste posing as bonds, CDOs, and other failing and illiquid credit instruments. He willfully ignored the obvious—and when Fannie and Freddie were nationalized by Uncle Sam, wiping out shareholders, his investors got creamed.

(Continued)

Q2. You said this was simple and not time-consuming, but that is you. I am new to options and new to looking at the world through dark glasses. Do you really think it is this simple?

If I didn't think you could do it—simply—I would not write this book. Writing this kind of book, barring all my neighbors buying 10,000 copies for their closest friends, pays about 6 cents an hour. But I love what I do, I have made tons of dough for my subscribers, and I feel many people truly need to diversify their portfolios and add short positions. And I know they can do it.

Let me give you a highly personal example: my wife. She and I both love Starbucks—the coffee, the service—and I once owned the stock. My kids still do—Bar Mitzvah presents from a friend who knows they manage their own portfolios. My wife came home one day and announced she was buying less coffee—and noticed her two favorite stores had lighter traffic than was usual. My amateur wife—she doesn't do stocks although she understands markets and the economy—was right and even took a look at the stock after she told me about her concerns. If she had spent another hour, maybe two, looking at comments, maybe calling a friend about their coffee-drinking habits, she would have gained the conviction to buy a put.

You can do it, too.

Q3. PFE was a great example. How do I find great ideas to begin this kind of analysis?

Great question, with no precise answer available. I do the following:

- *I subscribe* to several long newsletters and sites that give me ideas for the short side—when one company is successful it may come out of the profits of another.
- *I read many websites and blogs*—Seekingalpha.com and like that—and they are useful.
- *I look at my personal life*—I go to shopping malls and stores and home-building sites. For example, besides the general downturn in consumer spending that affects travel, I noticed what a pain in the neck it was to change a reservation via Expedia, my favorite travel site. I began price shopping on Expedia and then booking directly on a hotel or airline site. I asked around and many other people were doing it—and then a ChangeWave Research survey confirmed this trend. But it all began when I was put on hold during a busy day for too long a period of time.

Rules

- Your target price for a put should be either a double—a 100 percent gain—or whatever you are comfortable with.
- Don't be the first one in.
- Never average down.
- The simplest way to identify an opportunity is to find a disconnect between the company story and your view of reality.
- Set time stops—the time stop is a self-imposed inflection point.
- Cult stocks like Palm and Sun Microsystems can exist on air for years because they have cash and a history even if their market share shrinks and their prospects dim.
- The simplest way is to look at a chart of money flows and compare it to a chart of the stock market in general.
- Be mindful of deadly surprises—always.
- The price is the driving factor in selecting the right put.

Going Short the Traditional Way or Borrower Beware

I do not recommend that individuals ever short a stock the traditional way—borrowing shares, selling them, then buying them back when they are cheaper to repay the loan—but it would be silly to write a book called *Selling Short* without discussing selling short.

A Little History

Short selling has been reviled until very recently. Why?

From an emotional point of view, people hate people who in turn hate something they like—and short sellers supposedly hate a company or market, and want them to go down, while we all love stocks and markets and want them to go up. From a more practical point of view, short sellers hit stock prices—and often drive them down, in a small or big way, depending on how many short sellers there are—because they dump shares as soon as they borrow them.

Do I exaggerate about how disliked short sellers are through history?

The first famous short seller may have been Isaac Le Maire, a wealthy merchant. At the beginning of the 17th century he shorted stocks, notably the Dutch East India Company. After the Dutch stock market crashed in 1610, the government, naturally, outlawed short selling. This set a precedent—Napoleon declared short selling "treason" against the state as it inhibited his ability to raise money for his many wars. And it is not just Europeans who hated shorts—short selling was illegal in the good old U.S. of A. until 1850. And attitudes have not changed in many parts of the world—as recently as 1995 Malaysia, in the form of the Finance Ministry, proposed short sellers be caned.

In September 2008, first British authorities and then the SEC temporarily banned the shorting of financial stocks, and other markets took note. Soon other national regulatory authorities began to ban shorting of all or selected parts of their stock markets. This is not the place to discuss the politics of these bans, but simply put, they are counterproductive—shorting in modern markets is a critical component of movement and pricing of stocks and indices. The lack of short sellers distorts prices of stocks, options, and indices, prevents markets from making bottoms, and in the United States was unnecessary. When the SEC first announced a 10-day ban in September 2008, the short positions in financial stocks were actually smaller than in July.

How Shorting Works

Shorting is actually quite simple.

Step 1: You get a good idea about a bad company and you call your broker. She says they don't have shares of Shulman Media but they are easy to find, and they are. In less a few minutes, she has the 1,000 shares you want to short. These are shares held on behalf of clients by other brokerage houses. She tells you the interest rate you will be charged is 10 percent. The stock is selling for $20 at the time so you will be paying an annual rate of 10 percent on $20,000.

Step 2: You sell the stock as soon as you get it. If you are smart this is all being done in a separate account. The money from the sale stays in that account, not earning interest.

Step 3: A quarter later, people are really tired of Shulman Media— and Shulman, probably—and the stock has moved down to $10. You buy shares with the cash in this account, repay the loan of shares, and three month's interest or $500. You net $9,500.

Or . . .

The stock moves up over the course of the quarter and ends the quarter at $30 a share. Your broker calls and warns you if it goes above $30, you will start getting margin calls. The brokerage house is conservative and on a short position will only let you margin one-third of your obligation—and assumes your liability is what you have to pay to buy back the shares at the end of the day. Most brokers use traditional margin requirements of 50 percent, which means you need to meet margin calls at $40 a share.

Or . . .

The company is acquired for $80 a share and you will be out $80,000.

And that is it. Oh, I forgot—a tip on **how to cover.** Believe it or not, you can end up owning a stock and shorting it if you are not careful with your instructions to your broker. **When you call or go online to cover a short position, specify this purchase is to cover the open short position.** If you do not, you can end up buying the shares, having them sit in your account, and also have an open short position. Online brokerage services that allow for short positions manage this problem by asking if your purchase is to cover an open position.

Advantages and Disadvantages of Shorting

Some investors may see advantages with traditional shorting compared to what I prefer, buying puts.

Advantages

- **A Much Greater Universe:** Thousands of stocks trade that do not have put options, or puts that are not liquid. If you want to short them, you have to short them.

Albany Molecular Research

If there ever was a stock I should have shorted, rather than looking for a put, it was Albany Molecular Research (AMRI). As I was doing research into the impact of generic Claritin on the drug market, our surveys showed all branded and expensive antihistamines would take a hit. I looked around and saw that all the other big brands were held by diversified pharma companies. And then a colleague said he thought some company held a royalty on Allegra. A quick Google search told me a contract research organization, Albany Molecular Research (AMRI) did get a royalty on every sale of Allegra and these royalties were actually more than 100 percent of profits—if I

(Continued)

remember correctly at one time they were 140 percent of profits. Management was using these royalties to buy business—CROs compete for business based on cost and they were subsidizing new business. I looked and found that there were few puts available, they were highly illiquid, and the only way to play the downside was to short the stock, something ChangeWave's institutional clients may or may not have done. The stock was cut in half over a two-year period and a traditional short position would have produced great returns.

- **Volatility: Short positions are inherently less volatile than put positions,** especially for stocks investors see as a longer-term opportunity.
- **Position Management:** When shorting, investors can better use sell stops and price targets due to this reduced volatility.
- **No Premiums:** Short positions do not require investors pay for the time value of the position or the volatility embedded in put premiums. Simply put, short positions do not decay over time and lose or gain premium based on the volatility of the underlying stock. The only value an investor loses, over time, is the interest cost for the borrowed shares or, if margin dollars are being used, margin interest as well.

Disadvantages

- **Risk:** The single biggest disadvantage of shorting a stock in the traditional manner is unbelievable risk—a traditional short position can lead to financial ruin. In a long position, the most you can lose is 150 percent of your investment if you borrowed on margin to leverage your investment. **With a short position involving the borrowing of the stock, your theoretical potential loss is unlimited.** If you borrow a stock when it is at $10, and the stock goes to $200, you are out $190 a share—19 times your original investment! With shorting, investors have an open-ended liability as a stock rises.
- **Costs:** Transaction costs, including interest on borrowed shares, are higher than with put positions—and vary based on the difficulty of borrowing shares. Ongoing transaction and interest costs are unpredictable if the owner of the shares

sells them, forcing the short seller to replace these shares at potentially higher interest rates.
- **Taxes:** You cannot enjoy long-term capital gains treatments for profits.

Other Issues with Shorting

Brokers are able to handle most shorting requests. Going short is a little more complicated than going long, and buying puts and LEAPS is no different than buying calls and long-side LEAPS. That said, there are some major issues you need to understand before going short. Most of these issues relate to the actual shorting of a stock, not buying a put or a LEAPS.

- **The Margin Account:** You need to open a margin account to short a stock. It is in this account that the funds from your sale of borrowed stock will be placed. But don't count on the interest—not only will the broker charge you interest on the shares you borrowed, unless you are Warren Buffet or the CEO's cousin, they will not pay you interest on the funds in the account or sweep it into a money market fund.
- **Finding the Stock:** You may want to short a stock that is hard to find. The process of finding shares is called a "locate." If your broker cannot find them, you cannot short the stock. Some stocks are hard to short because their shares are not easily available to borrow, for a variety of reasons. And if you find it hard to find the shares, it also means there is either a large short position in the stock already or the stock is not held by a large number of individual shareholders, which means it is less liquid than trading statistics may indicate. It is also virtually impossible to short a stock with a price under $5, and you cannot short a stock within a specified period after its IPO, depending on the exchange.
- **Margin Calls:** If the price of the stock you have shorted rises, your broker will ask you to put more funds in this account, typically enough to cover the purchase of the stock on the open market at the current price. If you don't make the payment asked for by your broker, and you have other securities held long in that margin account, the broker will sell those securities to meet the margin call.

- **Early Sale:** If the original owner decides to sell the stock, you must replace it, either by finding other shares through your broker or buying it on the open market.
- **The Short Squeeze:** You have probably heard this term more often than you care to remember. A short squeeze is a market event in a stock when the price of a stock rises quickly, prompting shorts to cover—buy the stock in the open market to repay the shares they have borrowed. This in turn generates higher prices, which in turn prompts more people to sell and take a profit, which in turn has brokers calling more loans, which in turn forces many short sellers to go into the open market to cover their loans. And so on. Short squeezes can be ferocious, can last quite a while, and can be very expensive.
- **Interest Payments:** You will pay interest on the borrowed shares at the broker loan rate based on the price of the stock when you borrowed it.
- **Dividends:** If you have borrowed and shorted a dividend-paying stock, you will receive the dividends but you, in turn, must pay the original owner the value of the dividends.

Qualifying Yourself

Given the level of risk with the borrowing of shares, you need to qualify yourself to see if you should short any stock before you short a stock. I am not qualified—I am too risk averse. I would rather be wiped out on a put position than manage an open-ended liability. If you think you are—and I am not going to get into psychological profiling to see if you should do this—here are some simple rules:

- How hard is it for you to take losses? If you know this is a weakness, shorting may be dangerous for your financial—**and mental**—health.
- Do you have the capital for margin calls?
- Do you have the discipline to set and live by stop loss prices and target prices?

Anything more than that and I will need a license or get a call from Dr. Phil. **The key to traditional shorting is emotional discipline**

combined with a lack of ego. You need both to successfully short a stock. And you also need to avoid playing the market this way if you are "attracted to it" for reasons other than making money.

In 1987 I had a stock broker with the improbable name of Rodney Madrid—Rodney, you out there reading my book?—a great guy who introduced me to options trading, which pushed me, after some wonderfully big wins, toward this career. One day, Rodney called to ask if I wanted to short some overblown little stock the branch of his brokerage had access to that he thought would blow up soon. Sort of the inverse of the guys in *Boiler Room* (great movie) except he and his brokerage house were both legit. I had no idea what he was talking about, he was too excited to explain it properly, and I let it go. The next day the stock blew up and lost more than 80 percent of its value and I could hear Rodney dancing when he called to tell me.

When to Short Rather Than Buy a Put

When should you short stock versus buy a put?

As I said, never.

Create and Manage a Short Position

Regardless of whether you borrow shares and sell short or buy puts, there is no difference in identifying a prospective short. That said, after you decide to short a stock, the creation and management of that short position is quite different than when you buy a put.

- **Targets:** Targets should be set before the position is created. Although there is no rule of thumb that applies to thousands of stocks, the important thing is to set targets. I urge investors who buy puts to play defense first, be conservative, but when they establish a put position to go for home runs and 100 percent gainers. A 100 percent profit in a short position means the company has gone bankrupt—unlikely for most short opportunities, so **set firm price targets and cover when you hit them.**
- **Sell Stops: You must use the equivalent of sell stops to set automatic targets for when you will cover position**—either with a profit or a loss. Only you can determine how much you can lose. Ditto for profits—as part of setting sell stops

you need to predetermine how much margin you are willing to commit to a position to keep it alive.

- **Technical Indicators:** The number of shares held short and the days to cover are very important—you don't want to have daily margin calls during a short squeeze.
  - Avoid the outright shorting of a stock if the number of shares held short is 15 percent or more of the float and/or the days to cover are more than 10.
  - Check charts to see if, in the past, the stock has gone up temporarily on bad news—this will give you an indication if the stock suffers from short squeezes.
- **Avoiding Disaster:** Before opening a position you must:
  - Determine there are no discernible upside catalysts that could prompt the stock to rise very quickly—more than 30 percent—in a short period of time.
  - When there is little if any possibility the company can be acquired.
- **Capital Allocation:** Don't laugh—assume you will lose double the money you get into a short position. What, with my having set up the equivalent of sell stops? Assume your broker goes on vacation and the online broker you are using had technical problems and your sell stop does not exist.

Conclusion

This is one of the shortest chapters in the book—pardon the pun—due to the relative simplicity of shorting and my unwillingness to recommend actually shorting stocks through the borrowing of shares. That said, this is sometimes the only way to make money when a stock goes down.

Some of you may be up to it or may already be doing it. If so, good luck—and be as disciplined as you have ever been when investing in the market.

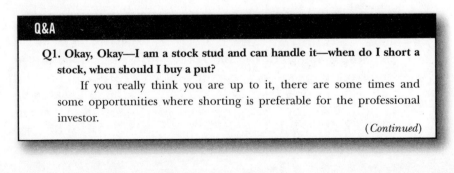

Q&A

Q1. Okay, Okay—I am a stock stud and can handle it—when do I short a stock, when should I buy a put?

If you really think you are up to it, there are some times and some opportunities where shorting is preferable for the professional investor.

(Continued)

- When there are no puts on the stock or the puts are not liquid—outstanding contracts are less than 3,000 in number.
- When put premiums are excessive—momentum or other considerations make the premiums on puts so excessive it is not possible to hit a home run and the basic risk/reward ratio is unfavorable compared to shorting the stock outright.
- When the spreads between Ask and Bid are unreasonable. This may mean short-term traders have hijacked options trading on a stock and a short position provides significantly better value if the stock declines as expected towards a target price.
- When portfolio or other requirements mean volatility must be kept to a minimum.
- When an investor has a system using targets and stop losses for long positions that you believe will work on short positions as well.

Q2. Why do authorities get so upset about shorting?

Simple—if a stock is cratering, and shorts pile in, dumping the stock as soon as they get it accelerates the downturn—which makes them a profit. During a massive run on a stock short selling can self-generate profits.

Q3. Have you ever shorted a stock?

No. And I never will.

Rules

- Rule #1: Don't short a stock—buy a put.
- With a short position involving the borrowing of the stock, your theoretical potential loss is unlimited.
- Thousands of stocks trade that do not have put options, or puts are not liquid. If you want to short them, you have to short them.
- Short positions are inherently less volatile than put positions.
- When shorting, investors can better use sell stops and price targets due to this reduced volatility.
- When you call or go online to cover a short position, specify this purchase is to cover the open short position.
- The key to traditional shorting is emotional discipline combined with a lack of ego.
- Set firm price targets and cover when you hit them.
- You must use the equivalent of sell stops to set automatic targets for when you will cover position.
- Avoid the outright shorting of a stock if the number of shares held short is 15 percent of the float or more and/or the days to cover are more than 10.
- Read Rule #1 again.

CHAPTER 8

Shorting a Market Segment

Other than the slam dunk, so obvious it hurts trade based on a known fact—such as Lipitor coming off patent—my favorite short position is playing a segment. This love affair—I like to get carried away—is due to the incredible data provided by ChangeWave Research surveys that put me ahead of Wall Street as to how a segment, industry, or the economy is going to do. And other data from other sources is readily available to make this, perhaps, your favorite kind of short position.

A short on a market segment is also the least risky position you can put on but still have the potential for a home run.

Identify a Segment

There are several ways to **create an initial prospect list** and identify a market segment to short—and they closely follow the methods, previously discussed, to identify individual stocks.

1. **Use a Peter Lynch approach:** Use your instincts. You can start your search by using your own observations about the world around you. As mentioned previously, I was in a Ruby Tuesday and saw a bunch of people using coupons and the bar was empty—the bar generates the most profitable part of any restaurant's business. I walked across the parking lot and saw that Bennigan's was even emptier (a few months later it went into bankruptcy, Chapter 7 or liquidation, in August 2008). The rest is history, the best short ever in my service, a position in Ruby Tuesday that returned more than 500 percent.

2. **Use data not used or misunderstood by Wall Street:** Wall Street does not have a monopoly on wisdom—or data. And finding data you find effective, more effective than what Wall Street relies on, can be a great road to profit. For example, most Wall Street analysts in 2007 and 2008 based their view of construction activity on official government statistics. And this data showed only a small slowdown in employment in construction, which on its face was absurd. I checked out the companies processing payments from the U.S. to Mexico and saw that growth had slowed from 35 percent to 10 percent at one outfit. My logic was simple: a slowdown in transfer payments was an indication that many of the undocumented workers serving the construction sector were out of work, the sure sign of a slowdown.

3. **Trade against headlines:** Hysteria creates bubbles in market segments that then become ripe for a spectacular fall. In the fall of 2001, the anthrax attacks on the Postal Service and Capitol Hill created a near instant bubble in any company remotely related to detecting or countering biological threats, from vaccine makers to bug detectors. These stocks soared and crashed and a patient trader could see this happening by the intensity of the headlines—and the more intense, the better the eventual opportunity.

4. **Lunch with people smarter than you are and knowledgeable of a segment:** This a great way to begin prospecting positions on the long or the short side. In this case, it was a broker/money manager who manages several hundred million dollars and has a partner that does research, with one focus in early 2007 being the housing market. In February of that year, at the cost of a nice lunch (a great Caesar salad if I remember correctly), I was pointed in a direction that produced winner after winner after winner. That year the market called four or five false bottoms among the home builders and my recommendations were very successful, thanks to that 90-minute conversation.

5. **Look for the hidden trade:** Often when the fundamentals of a segment are sliding there is collateral damage to companies dependent on or serving that market. When car sales in developing countries slid, demand for platinum for catalytic converters declined; when the Atkins craze faded, demand for eggs fell.

Hidden Trades

Hidden trades really do exist and individuals can find them—often ahead of Wall Street. Change-Wave Research and other data showed a coming slowdown in the purchasing of computer equipment by companies in the telecom and the financial sectors, simply confirming a consensus Wall Street view that an overall slowdown in capital spending was occurring due to problems in these sectors. Sun Microsystems had an outsized share of its revenues linked to these two sectors—you could get this information simply by reading Sun's quarterly reports or listening to their conference calls. That was enough for me: Sun was a slowly dying company I had shied away from shorting because it is also a cult stock that brings in money flows whenever the stock goes down a bit. But this coming softness from two core customer sets would, I felt, push away these rescue investors and the stock would fall. When the company discussed the weakness among buyers in a quarterly earnings announcement that disappointed the Street—poof—the stock cracked and the position returned exactly 100 percent, a pure double, in seven weeks. A classic hidden trade.

It is important you do not draw hasty or the wrong conclusion about an entire segment from an experience with one company. For example, if the local Chevrolet dealer has a glut of used cars, that does not mean CarMax or AutoZone is having problems (as I write this they are, by the way). Or if you find prices falling at one hotel chain on Expedia or their company website, you better check out several other hotel chains before you think the entire segment is having problems.

Looking at Segment Data

Go get more coffee, there is more work to do. Not much, but you need to look at segment data. Where to start? There are three kinds of data.

1. **Data you can find or interpret very quickly:** Nothing super elaborate. They are useful in helping develop a position against a segment. Most of it is easy to obtain by using sources you are already comfortable with or with simple searches in Google or Yahoo.
2. **Data you currently use for identifying and managing long positions. Stay within your comfort to zone**.
3. **Data used by Wall Street.** This is very easy to find. Zillions of websites publish this kind of data and even give you advance

notice of this data: Barrons.com, Economy.com, and Briefing.com come to mind. Or after you have identified a potential market segment, you can find these data sets by doing quick searches on Google or Yahoo. For example, let's say that you want or are shorting the retail sector and you want to look at government retail sales data, published monthly. Read a couple of articles summarizing past findings, if they were at, above, or below expectations, and then check the movement of some ETFs such as the XLY when this data broke. You will see how this data can move markets.

3. **Find proprietary, collateral, obscure, or other data that Wall Street ignores.** I mentioned this before but let me repeat: Go and find a data set that you understand that Wall Street does not. Some investors use information in paid services; a great deal of information is available free on the Web. Let me use an example that made people a lot of money. Official government and industry statistics showed new residential construction fell below the one million annual rate in early 2008. Historical data said that meant the segment had hit bottom. I said no way. I created a synthetic "new home" number—the number of newly built units plus the number of foreclosed homes minus the historical average for foreclosures. This is a realistic number because most foreclosed homes are pretty new. That synthetic number told me the number of new and near new homes being made available was almost as high as the rate seen at the peak of the housing bubble. And all of this was easy-to-find public information. You can find your own with a little bit of work.

Quick Tip—Quick Data from Seekingalpha.com

Seekingalpha.com is the largest financial blog in the world—it is actually a portal to a zillion blogs, most of them high quality (including my own) and is a great place to find segment data and to find analysts' predictions for a specific market segment. You may not find all the data you want but the site is often the first step in a thread that will take you where you want to go. Ditto for analysts' opinions. For example, I am not a client of Dick Bove's but I pretty much know what he has said soon after it comes out due to seekingalpha.com.

Market Makers and Breakers

No matter how smart you are, and no matter how dumb many on Wall Street often prove to be, you are not circulating reports, speaking at conferences, and appearing on CNBC. Simply put, certain **Wall Street analysts can make or break stocks and this is also true for moving an entire market segment**—while there may be many voices that speak about individual stocks, each segment has but a small group of analysts who can really move all the stocks within that segment.

The best example of this in recent months—perhaps a year and a half—is the power of Meredith Whitney to move financial stocks. I met Ms. Whitney on the set at Fox Business in 2007 on Halloween, the day the financial stocks broke, a few days after she put out a sell recommendation on Citigroup, stating they would have major write-offs and would have to cut their dividend. (For her honest opinion she was treated to death threats.) Whitney quickly became a media star and was made head of equity research at Oppenheimer. As I write this, I will stop and turn up the volume on CNBC or Fox if and when she is on—and I encourage you to do the same as you read this—because she is almost always right.

How do you follow analysts like Whitney? Simple. Go to Google, create an account, and sign up for Google news alerts for analysts you consider important for segments you have interest in or you are shorting.

Meredith Whitney

If you ever plan on shorting the financial sector you had better know Meredith Whitney. No one has been more correct—astonishingly so—in the two-plus years since the credit markets began to wobble and her work has value for anyone interested in the financial sector in the foreseeable future. Her role in forecasting the financial stock meltdown is described to perfection by Michael Lewis in the December 2008 edition of *Portfolio* magazine. I met Ms. Whitney on the set of Fox Business in October 2007—Halloween, the day the short side music started and investors began playing musical chairs and picking losers in the financial sector. This was two days after she received death threats for recommending Citigroup stock be sold and predicting the company would cut its dividend (which it eventually did). Her work is invaluable, emphasizing a macro view of credit and financial markets while explaining why specific companies will or have a problem. When she puts out a new report—one that is negative or positive—financials can move down as much as 5 percent or more. Citigroup went from near $40 to under $5 within a year of her recommendation to sell the stock.

Determining the Best Segments

Let me be very clear and careful with what the term "best" means—the best segments to short typically trade as a group, and ETFs are available that reflect the segment and are easily shorted by individuals. The word best does not mean these are the best segments to short as you read this.

The best segments have several things in common.

First is a **track record of moving as a group** when sentiment changes on Wall Street. You can check this by taking several major names in a segment and charting them together. This is easy to do on Yahoo; see Figure 8.1. For example, you would draw the one- or two-year chart of Pfizer, Merck, Schering Plough, GlaxoSmithKline, and a few other Big Pharma outfits if you wanted to see if this segment moves as a group—and, as it turns out, it does not, which many would find surprising.

Second, look for segments with **"long" Exchange Traded Funds (ETFS) available for this segment.** When evaluating a segment the availability of ETFs that properly represent the segment and where you can buy puts that are liquid is quite important. New ETFs pop up every day—there are several websites you can check out to see what is new. You should check out the components of these ETFS—the stocks they hold—for sometimes they do not really mirror the

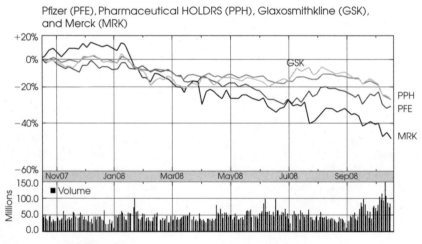

Figure 8.1   The Segment Moves

Source: CSI Data

part of a market segment you think is weakening. There are ETFs that move one for one with a market segment or ultratype ETFs that move at a rate double that of the underlying market segment.

Also look for **segments with Short Exchange Traded Funds.** This is a relatively new class of ETFs that are already short—you do not buy puts on these ETFs, you either buy the ETF itself or you buy calls on the ETF if you want extra leverage. They are popping up every week and enable investors to go short a segment without shorting a stock or buying a put. There are two flavors: the Short ETF, which moves up $1 as each dollar of stocks it is shorting loses a dollar in value, or the double-short ETF, which goes up $2 for every dollar the underlying stocks go down.

There are **negative indicators** and data points you need to include in your analysis of a segment. One is **the market leader effect**—a market leader (Intel within semiconductors comes to mind) may have outsized success or performance that pulls up the entire segment even though that segment is in trouble. Big cap biotechs fall into this category; one big data point for a Biogen or Genentech can move the entire segment for a few days. Look at Figure 8.2, which shows how the semiconductor sector (the SOXX) and Intel often move in parallel.

Another negative is **lots of M&A activity**—industries and segments periodically go through consolidation and this artificially drives up prices of shares as investors speculate on the next takeover or merger. Often the valuations of companies in a segment hit by M&A move up based on the last acquisition price.

ETFs

What exactly is an ETF? They are securities that look like index funds—mutual funds that track market indices—but trade like the shares of individual stocks. Legally, they are far different. ETFs when created are not sold directly to investors. The company or sponsor offering the ETF issues large blocks of what are called creation units, often more than 50,000 or 100,000 at a time. These creation units in turn are purchased by industry insiders such as a market maker, an exchange specialist, or a large institutional investor such as a hedge fund. These folks then put the creation units in a trust. That trust goes out and buys the underlying shares of the ETF. The creation units are then split up and sold to you and me and they function as a share of the underlying securities in the trust.

Figure 8.2   The Market Leader Effect

Source: CSI Data

Also look for the segment's **sensitivity to exogenous factors.** Some segments are clearly sensitive to exogenous factors you may not be able to predict when building a position. For example, even though the economy is declining as I write this and shipping companies such as FedEx and UPS are natural shorts because of their direct correlation to economic activity; their share prices are also tightly tied to oil prices given the importance of the cost of fuel to their businesses. I have avoided shorting them for this reason—and as I watch oil prices go down and their share prices rise even though the economy is slipping, I am happy about my caution.

And, as always, **watch out for government and politics.** New government action can wreck or boost a position. In the fall of 2007 I recommended shorting the very low end discount stores as ChangeWave surveys showed folks on the lowest end of the income scale—the typical customers of these stores—were getting hit hard by gas prices and rising unemployment. Then, as politicos began to talk about a tax rebate and relief package, I closed the positions as this would pump money directly into this customer set. The timing was good—profits were more than 100 percent for several of these positions when I recommended closing them and soon thereafter the shares rose due to the rebate program. So keep an eye on Uncle Sam—for good or for bad for your short positions.

Ways to Short—"Long" ETFs

Financial innovation has given individual investors a great many new tools to short discrete market segments, notably Exchange Traded Funds. **ETFs are not the only vehicle for shorting a segment but the best place to start.** The first group are **long ETFs**—you would buy a put on these ETFs—and there are, as I write this, lots of them, more than 700 ETFs ranging from agricultural suppliers (a great symbol, MOO) to gold. Before plunging in when you see that an ETF exists for a segment you want to short, some basic homework is in order.

- **Components: You need to evaluate components of the ETF.** All ETFs have components—underlying stocks—and sometimes the name or focus of the ETF is out of sync with your view of the market segment. For example, Chinese ETFs, both long and short, do not mirror mainland Chinese markets, they mirror Chinese ADRs, the Hong Kong market, and companies with heavy exposure to China. This information is available either at the site of the company offering the ETF, such as Proshares.com or at general financial sites such as Yahoo.com. If something does not look correct to you—if it is out of alignment with your understanding of the market segment—move on.
- **Liquidity:** You need to check out the liquidity—the trading volume—of the ETF and the availability and trading volume of puts on this ETF. A lack of liquidity means, a) the puts will be more expensive due to relatively large spreads between the ask and the bid, and, b) if there is a big event these spreads might widen in your favor if it is bad news or widen against you if good news hits. **Look for daily trading volume in the underlying ETF of at least 250,000 shares.** Also **look for liquidity in puts** as measured by the number of calls and puts—together—outstanding. There is a debate on what this number should be. I think **you need to see at least 5,000 puts outstanding in a given month.** One caveat: option buyers often move from one month to the next, so if the closest in month has more than 5,000 contracts outstanding, and later months that are of interest to you have less than 5,000

contracts, you may still want to consider these as some short term money will move into later months as time goes by.

- **Technical indicators:** You should look at all the same momentum and other technical indicators you would review when **targeting a stock** and creating a put position on an individual stock.
- **Target Prices:** Target prices are harder to set because of the nature of an ETF—it contains many companies—and target prices are best created using charts and other technical indicators, a cruder but necessary tactic. There are no tested rules of thumb I can offer here—but ETFs follow most of the patterns of individual equities.

I would keep it simple with an emphasis on changes in the put/call ratio—more put buying is obviously a good sign—and the 50-day moving average. If an ETF is below its 50-day MA and cannot break through, you should create a target price that assumes another leg down for the segment and your target price should be set accordingly.

Ways to Short—Short ETFs

This is a relatively new class of ETFs—short and ultra- or double-short ETFs. **Short ETFs are an individual short seller's dream,** an ETF that shorts a particular segment of the market such as financials. They are actually called "Inverse ETFs." In the first half of 2008 the money invested in these inverse ETFs more than doubled. In the summer of 2008 they constituted only 3.5 percent of all investment in ETFs but 13 percent of daily trading volume.

There are two kinds: **the single short ETF**—it aims to go up 1 percent when a market segment goes down 1 percent, and the double or what are generically known as ultra- or **double-short ETFs** that go up 2 percent when the segment goes down 1 percent. For the more aggressive investor these ETFs offer the ultimate rocket-fueled trade—buying calls on a double-short segment ETF.

- **Buying A Short ETF:** As with other ETFs, you need to evaluate components, liquidity, and technical indicators, and when possible you should check to see if the ETF is tracking directly against a long-only ETF for its segment. Go to Yahoo and chart them. This takes about five seconds—and if there is a noticeable difference in performance, check out the components—and one or the other may have a better basket of components that fits your view. For example, XLF is a long ETF for the financial segment; SEF is the short ETF for the same segment. If you look at the charts for these two ETFs, they do not track the way they should—they are not perfect mirrors of each other, at least in the period of time when I am writing—and it would be better and you would have made more profits by buying the puts on the XLF than to buy the SEF.

A variation of the short ETF is the double-short ETF—a short ETF on steroids. These ETFs are for more aggressive investors, for as they produce twice the gains in a segment when that segment falls, they also produce twice the losses when that segment moves up. Look at Figure 8.3 to see how the double-short ETF for the financial sector, the SKF, inversely mirrors, with much more bang, the long ETF for that sector, the XLF.

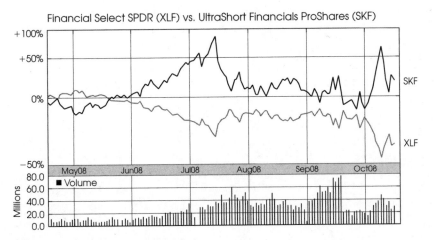

Figure 8.3 Financial ETFs: Long and Short

Source: CSI Data

A list of short ETFs would be out-of-date before the e-mail went to my editor. They are easy to find via various financial websites or by doing simple searches on Yahoo or Google.

- **Buying Calls on Short ETFs:** This is the equivalent of adding crack to the steroids. The underlying security can be a single-short or a double-short ETF, and you are then buying a call, not a put, that is a contract allowing you to buy the ETF at a fixed price at a future date. Calls are the inverse of puts and you can super-speculate on the decline of a market segment.

  The leverage is remarkable even for just a morning of activity in the market. Let's say you wake up and the Dow is down modestly, 72 points. The financial sector, as measured by the XLF, is down 2.25 percent, a big move and exactly the same amount as the Dow Jones Financial Index. The SEF, the single-short ETF, is up only 1.3 percent; the SKF, the double-short ETF, is up 3.6 percent; the closest in the money calls on the SKF, the August $110s, are up 22 percent, and the nearest out-of-the-money calls are up more than 40 percent. Translation: A slightly more than 2 percent downturn in the segment led to a 40 percent plus rise for a call on a double-short ETF. That's leverage.

  This is a trade for the aggressive investor. And, a reminder: it works the other way as well. A 2 percent rise in the underlying market segment could lead to a 40 percent drop in the calls.

- **Selling Puts on Short ETFs:** A slightly more conservative way to get even more leverage on double-short and single-short ETFs is to sell puts on a double-short ETF.

  When you sell a put you are selling someone the right to "put" the stock or ETF to you at a given price. For example, the SKF is now at $114 and you sell an October $100 put, collecting $800 per contract. If in October the price of the ETF is above $100, the put will expire worthless. You have no obligation to buy the ETF itself.

  This is a trade many investors put on when they see something rising long term and are willing to actually buy the underlying ETF or stock when the stock is put to them because they are convinced the longer term trend is in their favor. There are limitations. For example, most brokers require you have enough cash in an account to cover the cost of the ETFs or stocks if they are put to you. But the returns can be compelling—the simple trade of selling $100 puts on the SKF returned 8 percent in two months, assuming you are right about the trade.

Ways to Short—The Position Basket

You can call this a **create-your-own mini-ETF** trade. Using this approach, an investor would buy puts on several (or more) companies in a market segment. Why use this approach?

- **A Basket Reduces Risk:** If the market segment turns up, a basket of five positions will probably see a mix of movements and not all stocks and puts will move as fast as the market segment itself. And the inverse is also true: A basket reduces the potential upside you might experience if a single stock and put position completely blows up in your favor.
- **The Market Leader:** Many investors like to play a segment through the market leader—Intel in semiconductors, Cisco in Internet infrastructure, Citigroup in banking, Wal-Mart in discount retailing. If you think the segment is weak or weakening, you play the leader because that one company inevitably goes down with the segment. One advantage is puts on huge market cap companies are typically liquid and the spreads between Bid and Ask are small, reducing the cost of getting into a trade. I am not a big fan of this approach, but it has made many investors a lot of dough.
- **The Market Loser:** Another approach is to find the worst or weakest company in a falling segment and use a put position in this company as your play on the segment. For example, when women's clothing weakened, I settled on Liz Claiborne and a series of rolled positions returned almost 700 percent while the segment was down just 11 percent in the same time period. If this is of interest to you, look at the components of segment indices and ETFs and see what companies lead—and are trailing. Produce some charts to see if and to what extent the market leader moves with the segment. Then go ahead and short them using the criteria I discussed before.

Conclusion

If I were allowed to short in only one fashion, I would short market segments using baskets of stocks, the worst company in the segment, and ETFs depending on the price, risk-reward ratio, and liquidity of their respective puts. When segments crash, they crash hard and present a great many opportunities among individual companies. For example, in the first half of 2008, the market was down 13 percent but many retailers were down 35 percent or more and banks more than 50 percent. Shorting any number of names or an ETF would have brought you great profits.

Q&A

Q1. You have said it is best not to be the first person in—the first investor to see a stock falling—is this also true for market segments?

Yes. And actually it is a bit easier to identify a shift in trend in a segment than an individual stock. Charts, headlines, analyst comments—they come out in much greater volume about a segment than an individual company. Also, segments that are falling typically move more slowly than a stock, giving you more time to get in after the trend has turned downward.

Q2. How risky is buying a call on a double-short ETF?

Very. But the risk-reward ratio is very favorable.

Let's say you buy an out-of-the-money call that expires three months out on a double-short ETF and the market segment moves against you that day or week by 3 percent to 4 percent. The call is going to get whacked, down maybe 50 percent. Why is this so? There is always a certain residual value in a call (or a put) that will hold up if the call has several months to go before expiration. But a similar move to the upside could produce 400 percent to 800 percent gains on an out-of-the-money call. That is a pretty good risk-reward ratio.

Q3. What are the potential consequences of buying a put that is fairly illiquid or in a fairly illiquid ETF?

One for sure—you will pay more for the put than if it were more liquid. The seller of almost anything has the advantage in these situations. Another potential problem: If you want to get out at specific time and price, even though you are a seller, you may find it more difficult because there are fewer buyers. The bottom line: Use limit orders all the time.

Rules

- A short on a market segment is also the least risky position you can put on but still have the potential for a home run.
- It is important you do not draw hasty or the wrong conclusions about an entire segment from an experience with one company.
- Certain Wall Street analysts can make or break stocks and this is doubly true for moving an entire market segment.
- The best segments to short trade as a group and where ETFs are available that reflect the segment and are easily shorted by individuals.
- Also look for segments with Short or Inverse Exchange Traded Funds.
- Look for the certain negative indicators that make shorting a segment too difficult—the market leader effect, lots of M&A activity, the segment's sensitivity to exogenous factors, and, as always, government and politics.
- ETFs are not the only vehicle for shorting a segment but the best place to start.
- You need to evaluate components of the ETF.
- Look for daily trading volume in the underlying ETF of at least 250,000 shares.
- You need to see at least 5,000 puts outstanding in a given month.
- You should look at all the same momentum and other technical indicators you would review when targeting a stock.
- Short ETFs are an individual short seller's dream.

Creating the Great Segment Trade

You pull out your shotgun and look for a barrel with some fish in it and lo and behold, you find the U.S. financial sector. Let's short the financials. I mean, let's use this segment as an example of how to short a segment. I am not suggesting you walk out of the book store and short financials. Let's walk through two trades—the short on the segment through the purchase of a put on the ETF, and let's do a rocket-fueled trade.

Prospecting

The rules of keeping it simple and common sense still apply.

The banks are weak and weakening. The news is everywhere from the *Wall Street Journal* to the latest fortune you received in a cookie at the local Chinese restaurant. You troll around reading and prospecting in a manner similar to the way you identify and prospect individual companies. You see that, collectively, financial institutions have written off more than $400 billion in bad loans—and the headlines and the IMF believe it will become a trillion.

You let your dog analyze several investment banks' balance sheets and he barks it has negative equity. Meredith Whitney has just downgraded the darling of the industry, Goldman Sachs, and is talking about a pullback in lending of $2 trillion this year and more than that next year, which means $4 trillion in fewer assets to be used to generate profits.

You confirm all this data with another exquisite Caesar Salad and the broker you know who knows the banks and financial institutions as well as anyone in your universe. She tells you to look at them all, large and small, regional and national, money center and investment banks.

Time to go for it.

Segment Data

Banking data is almost too easy too find. There are an enormous number of data points to take into account. What are the best sets of data? Going back to simplicity and common sense, select the data that will drive this trade and if available in similar situations, drive other trades as well. Even if the data is overwhelming and clear cut, **don't skip any necessary steps for evaluating a target.**

The amount and negativity are overwhelming—not one analyst or researcher can produce positive data about the financial sector in general or a subsector in particular. The only optimistic voices are traders looking to move markets and long-only money managers, also a group of eternal optimists.

The CEOs of virtually every financial institution cannot say when the bottom in write-offs or earnings will happen. Neither can Ben Bernanke. If the CEOs of the nation's retailers said they could not predict next quarter's sales and earnings and the president said the growth rate for the economy was not predictable in the coming quarter, then you would think of shorting retail stocks.

Very quick math—the IMF and many others from respected research and brokerage shops believe write-offs will hit one trillion or more. A five second Google search shows write-offs to date equal $400 billion. So there are a lot more negative earnings announcements coming. If home inventories are at a 12-month supply when they are historically at a five-and-a-half month supply, you would begin considering shorting home builders. Simple math is good math.

That is enough. Time to go short.

Market Makers and Breakers

The leading market movers—Meredith Whitney, Bill Gross of PIMCO, and his compadre Mohamed El-Erian—all see more bad news ahead and Whitney has just cut estimates for virtually all the banks. If Mary Meeker had done the same during the Internet bubble, it was time to short Internet stocks.

Can the Segment Be Shorted?

This is one of if not the easiest segment to short—a critical component of any short position on an entire market segment. Why?

- There is a discrete and well-followed index for the segment—the Dow Jones U.S. Financial Services Index.
- There are multiple long ETFs that directly track—the iShares Dow Jones U.S. Financial Services Index Fund—or indirectly track the index such as the Financial Select Sector Spider or XLF. There at least 25 long ETFs; the XLF is by far the largest and most liquid long ETF.
- There are several short ETFs for this segment. Yeah! The ones to mention are the SEF—a one-for-one short ETF, and the SKF, the UltraShort Financials ProShares, which is designed to go up twice as fast as the market segment goes down.
- The larger long ETFs have puts—you can short them—and the SKF has calls if you want a rocket-fueled trade, buying a call on a double-short ETF.
- Investment banks trade as a group, money center banks trade as a group, regional banks trade as a group. You can verify this by checking out some charts. You can easily assemble a basket of positions—your own mini-short ETF—or play a market leader with a reasonable expectation of mirroring movement in the general segment.

Collateral Influences

One advantage you have when trying to reach a decision about the financial sector is a previous knowledge of the housing market in the U.S. You have been following problems with housing and the home builders for several months and had come to the conclusion that Wall Street had it wrong and many more defaults and foreclosures were coming. You also see a continuation of declining home prices as a driver in the decline of consumer confidence, spending, and the economy, and this in turn would lead to more defaults on credit cards and auto loans.

Negatives

Nothing is ever perfect. Even Babe Ruth struck out occasionally.

- **Short positions in many stocks and ETFs are large and growing** and the segment is prone to short covering, short squeezes, and massive short-covering rallies that can hurt positions in the short term. You look at some bad news headlines for Bear Stearns in the weeks before it blew up and notice it occasionally went up on bad news.
- **The government**—and even bland statements from government officials—can move the segment in either direction very quickly. Look what happened when Uncle Sam took over Freddie and Fannie. Even individual politicians can move markets. For example, Senator Chuck Schumer's note about possible problems at IndyMac led to a run on the bank and a meltdown in many other banks; Senator Chris Dodd's words about Fannie Mae made that stock move in the opposite direction for a while.

Picking the Tactic

Lots of choices—what to do, what to play? At the end of some serious thinking, you choose to put on, and I will walk you through, two trades.

Trade #1: Buy Puts on the XLF, the Financial Sector Spider. You like this trade because:

- **The XLF has been tracking the segment** quite closely and, for traders, is the benchmark ETF—it has more than $7 billion in assets, has the lowest turnover and the lowest volatility of any financial ETF—you can see this with a couple of clicks on Yahoo, nothing fancy or hidden here. This means spreads will be lower and puts more fairly priced when you buy them.
- **Puts are hugely liquid**, with **millions of contracts trading** each day. There are six possible expiration dates available, including LEAPS, which for very long investors (more than a year) offer preferential capital gains treatments.
- **The put/call ratio is increasing dramatically** in favor of puts—you have been watching this for a few days—and even

though the 50-day moving average is against us, the put/call ratio says momentum is on the side of the puts.

- **This trade has at least two months of clear sailing** from intrinsic or exogenous surprises. The financial institutions do not announce earnings for two more months, which means there are no potential upside revenue or earnings surprises lurking. Congress is out and everyone is campaigning or on vacation, so barring a meltdown there will be no meddling with this segment until after the election. Remember—**don't be afraid to shy away from a trade if you cannot get a double on a put position.**

Trade #2: A Rocket-Fueled Short on the Financials: Buying Calls on the SKF

- As you approached this segment, you felt the banks were a good target; by the time you finished even a cursory analysis, it was obvious they were the best opportunity in a long time and that the meltdown in stocks could take place over several quarters. That being said, there are also some short-term opportunities, which led you to be much more aggressive and put on a **much higher risk, higher reward trade** that could pay off in the short term.
- **The trade is to buy a call on the double-short ETF**—the SKF— the Ultrashort Financial ProShares ETF. Yup, you decide to take 2 percent of your trading account and be a pig—and accept the risk of potentially being slaughtered—and buy calls on a double-short fund. How piggish? On a day in the week of expiration of a call, the Dow Jones Financial Index is down 5.76 percent; the SKF is up 8.2 percent from $110 to $119; the calls you are looking at to get a feel for the trade—the $115 calls—are up 166 percent from $2.70 to $7.20. That, simply put, is leverage. And, as a reminder, you tell yourself, out loud, it also works the other way: Those calls would have been cut in half if the segment had moved in the other direction.

Selecting the Right Positions

You have chosen two trades: what strike prices and dates are appropriate for each one?

Trade #1: Puts on the XLF

You want at least six months and one earnings announcement before the puts expire.

Six months buys you time in case a relief rally—and they can happen at any time—punishes this position short term.

You want to own a put through one earnings announcement. The stocks may slide and the puts may increase greatly in value in anticipation of bad earnings.

Your two choices are the March 2009—seven months out—or the January 2010 and you quickly settle on the March 2009 as they have more leverage—there is more bang for the buck if the stocks melt down. Also, if you choose to roll the position—I will discuss this in Chapter 10—there are contracts further out.

At present the XLF is trading at $21.18. **You look for a price that is a mix between providing great leverage and being close enough to a possibility they may even get in the money.** Remember, positions are initially designed to hit home runs. The previous 12-month low is $16.72 so there is plenty of room to fall and still not make a new low. You opt for the $18 puts selling at $1.25. No need for a complicated Black-Scholes analysis—although you could have used any number of online tools to do so. The strike price is more than a buck above the previous low but the put is still fairly priced—$1.25. What this means is the XLF has to fall 15 percent for the put to break into the money, not a great distance, and you have seven months to see this happen.

You execute the trade and buy the March 2009 $18 puts for $1.25. The target price for the ETF is the previous low, $16.72, sometime after earnings are released in October and before the election, about two months from now. If that happens the put will be in the money. It will have a core value at that time of $1.28 and a time value, based on simple long division, of 20 cents (or a bit less) per month remaining for a total value of $2.28; a double, give or take, always the goal for a new position.

That previous low is the target but real profits might happen sooner. You assume the put will **decay** 20 cents per month (perhaps a bit less), so if the ETF hits $20 in a month, and stays out of the money, it may also trade for roughly $2.23, the current price ($1.25) plus the depreciation in the stock ($1.18) minus the time decay in the option ($0.20). The net is a 78 percent gain in a short period of time. You will use both these targets as you manage this position (next chapter).

Trade # 2: Calls on the SKF

There are not many choices here—a put two months out and one five months out. Put options expire on the third Friday of the month, which for the closer in month is the 17th. Citigroup and Bank of America announce earnings on the 16th of that same month; Lehman Brothers one month before. This makes you a bit nervous, but as you do not intend to hold these puts to expiration, you like the potential of hitting not just a home run but a grand slam and go for the closer in calls that expire in two months. You take one look at the price of these call options and **call off the trade.**

What happened?

The premiums on the calls border on the absurd. Let me tell you why.

Remember the previous low on the XLF was $16.72 or 21 percent lower than the current price. If the XLF, representing the financial sector, fell that much the SKF would increase 35 percent to 42 percent. This means the SKF would rise from its current level of $119 to $162–$170.

Currently the $170 calls are selling for $7.40. Yesterday they sold for $4.30, so these puts can move quickly. **They may be a great trade but . . .**

If the financial sector hits its previous low, and if you hold the puts until expiration, the trade does not work. You want a double, a 100 percent winner by expiration—on any trade, at a minimum— which means the call at expiration would have to be $185, and the sector would have to trade almost 10 percent below its previous low, a major technical resistance point you are not willing to butt heads with.

Bottom line: **no trade.**

You are not punking out, **you are showing much needed discipline, the kind you need to have if you are not going to lose your shirt.** Yes, if the segment drops another 5 percent to 10 percent in a few days—a real possibility—these calls could triple. But this should not matter—you are not a momentum trader, you build positions based on fundamentals. They are lousy for the banks but fundamentals often need time to play out. Remember the rules way back when—capital preservation, even when going for home runs, play defense until you see the great opportunity. This trade is simply too risky.

Getting Out

Getting out is simple—shoot for a double, a 100 percent gain—but be disciplined: Sell before the 100 percent target if need be and don't create a position if the math and logic do not work.

Conclusion

The method for establishing a target and establishing a position for a stock is similar to what you need to do to short a market segment. It may even be a bit simpler than with a stock because a troubled or falling segment will receive more attention in the media, there will be more supportive data and more analysts' opinion for you to scrutinize. There are also several more ways—in certain segments—to short a segment than simply buying a put.

Q&A

Q1. Did you really do a financial trade in your service similar to what you wrote about in this chapter?

Oh yes. After Meredith Whitney pointed me in that direction I spent some time looking at what was going on in the banking sector. I recommended many trades for my subs—almost all of them successful. My subs had to ride out a lot of short-covering rallies and volatility—but it paid off.

Q2. You said you tied the movement of a market segment with others? Should a trader play two segments she thinks are linked?

The focus on such an important segment pointed me to many other opportunities in consumer discretionary spending and home-building. The same is true for many segments, not just banking. For example, if there is a decline in retail spending you would automatically turn to travel and entertainment and do some research, and so on.

Rules

- Don't skip any necessary steps for evaluating a target.
- Don't be afraid to shy away from a trade if you cannot get a double, on a put position, if the underlying ETF hits its target price.
- Be disciplined—sell before the 100 percent target if need be and don't create a position if the math and logic do not work.

CHAPTER

10

Shorting the Indices—Only the Big Ones. Please.

Let me guess what you are thinking; let me put it in your own words. "I made a small fortune playing the indices going up, now I think they are going down and I want to do the same thing. How do I do it? Tell me all there is to know." Sorry, the variations in shorting indices would fill several books, this is just one chapter. But this chapter may not only make you a lot of money, it may save you a great deal of money as well.

Yes, you may be right, and we could now be, or someday be, in a secular bear market and short- and long-term short positions against the market could make you a lot of money. This chapter, however, sticks to the six-month rule for put positions I put forth in Chapter 4, and is more about how to go about shorting a market once you have made the determination it is going down. That said, you should short the general market when fundamentals are telling you the market should turn down, typically a falloff in corporate earnings. Here are some general principles and tactics that will (a) keep you from losing money, and (b) make you some money.

You should short the general market when fundamentals tell you the market should turn down, typically a falloff in corporate earnings. **You should invest against the market if you see a downturn coming, and not try to day-trade a market index—that is a different skill set.**

Trading on index movements is huge, liquid, and as you get more esoteric, the province of professional traders, not individual traders or investors. Large volumes for technical traders and many PhD dissertations have been written around trading market indices. I am going to stick to several simple methods for shorting market indices—the Dow Jones Industrial Average, the NASDAQ, and the S&P 500—and I emphasize, again, the importance of simplicity. I want to add to this mantra of simplicity the need to master a small number of trading methods rather than try to do too much.

Simplicity is critical to success—you should master one or just a few methods to play market movements. I have a friend who recently became a financial advisor based on his love of trading and his incredible success—he has turned $50,000 into $1.7 million over 14 years—and paying taxes on gains all along the way. How did he do this? Trading credit spreads—I will discuss this in Chapter 15. He uses a proprietary algorithm that in turns plays off volatility, but my point is that all he plays is the S&P 500 and for the most part all he does is trade based on one core method with some variations. His success is based on mastery of a core method of dealing with movements in the markets—and if you want to be active here, you should do the same.

The Major Indices

Hundreds of indices are created and maintained by the exchanges and research shops and serve as the basis for various trading instruments. What is interesting is how the preference of traders and investors affects the general use of indices—the more popular a type of option contract or futures product is, and the greater its liquidity, the more popular the index becomes rather than vice versa.

There are lots of indices. The ones I discuss in this chapter are for U.S. markets. And there are several ways to short them: options, futures, options on futures, and ETFs. With this in mind I want to focus on just a few indices that are simple and easy to trade:

- **The Dow Jones Industrial Average:** The DJIA is the grand-daddy of all indices (well, technically, the Dow Jones Transportation Average came first) and dates back to 1896. It is the most frequently cited index in the world. The DJIA leads all ticker symbols, is the first thing we hear when turning on financial news, and is the metric the general public uses to gauge the health of the stock market. It has 30 components—many of them nonindustrial companies—and is a price-weighted index that actually does not reflect the relative values of all its components. Translation: high-priced stocks carry more weight in the index than low-priced stocks so if $110 IBM moves 2 percent—$2.20—and $20 AT&T moves 2 percent—$0.40—the move of IBM has far more impact on the overall average even if AT&T had a larger market capitalization.

- **The S&P 500:** This is arguably the world's most popular investing and trading index, even though the Dow Jones Industrial Average is the first headline read at the end of the day. **The S&P 500 is considered—and is—more representative of corporate and economic performance than the Dow,** or any other index for that matter. The index comprises 500 of the largest corporations in the U.S. Investors can buy any one of a large variety of trading instruments—puts, futures, and so on—to play the S&P and most of these products are highly liquid. The S&P's most notable difference, day to day, from the Dow is its heaver weighting of financial stocks than the Dow Jones Industrial Average.

  While researching this book I visited, like a regular tourist, the Chicago Mercantile Exchange and Chicago Board of Options. Standing in the visitor gallery, at least 100 feet above this enormous trading floor more than the size of a football field, I was struck by how the glass wall separating the gallery from the pits kept out sound until the clock moved and the S&P futures pits opened—and you could hear the roar through the glass. This frenzy occurs every day, making the S&Ps the easiest and simplest places to invest against the general market.

- **The NASDAQ Composite:** This is the index quoted when commentators say the NASDAQ did this or the NASDAQ did that. It is a weighted average of all NASDAQ stocks with weights being determined by the market capitalization of the company—if Apple, with a market cap of $137 billion, goes up 2 percent, this moves the NASDAQ big time. If a little guy like Biocryst with a market cap of $118 million goes up 100 percent, it barely moves the index, if at all.

- **The NASDAQ 100:** This index comprises the 100 largest nonfinancial companies listed on the NASDAQ. This index can be traded in many ways, the most popular (average daily volume as I write this is 167 million) being something called the QQQs—the triple QQQs—the Powershares ETF for the NASDAQ 100. **The NASDAQ 100 is the index traders short when betting against technology companies.**

That is it—these are the general market indices you need to concern yourself with when considering a short of the general market. And when it comes down to actually shorting general markets, the list gets shorter.

When (and When *Not*) to Short the Market

I am not a market timer. In the past when I go long in a big way the market typically goes down, when I have shorted the market it goes up. Call me an inverse market timer—and this is the experience of many individual investors I have spoken with over the past few years. That being said, **there are times to short the general market.**
    When? Let's start with why.

- **Market timing:** You may be a market timer—good luck to you—and decide the market is going down for the next six days, six weeks, six months, whatever.
- **Hedging:** You are essentially long with most of your portfolio and you want to balance this out by shorting the market to protect your portfolio, in full or in part, against a market downturn.
- **Upcoming catalysts:** Many traders play the short side in anticipation of an upcoming catalyst, ranging from the earnings of a major company such as General Electric, a speech by the Chairman of the Fed, or the presidential election. Shorting the market around a catalyst is a trade—not an investment—but can be highly profitable when you are right. Markets often move in anticipation of a catalyst—"buy on the rumor, sell on the news"—and many traders exit positions before the actual catalyst or event occurs.
- **You are a secular bear:** You believe we are in a secular bear market and over time playing the downside of the general

market will be more profitable compared to playing individual short or long positions.

- **Technician:** You are a technician and see a downturn coming—why are you reading this book?

Back to when. Are there times that are better to short the market than others? Or times not to?

Time to Short

- **The 50-Day Moving Average:** As with individual stocks and ETFs, the 50-day moving average is a well-watched and influential gauge of trends in the market. **If you want to short the market do not do it when the moving average is moving up strongly** with a clear trend line.
- **New Highs versus New Lows:** Professional traders put tremendous emphasis on the number of stocks making new highs versus making new lows—and these traders move markets. This is a commonly reported statistic many reject as useful as it is a coincident indicator—a single data point does not a trend make. So, turn it into a trend line—**if there is a steady trend showing new lows outpacing new highs,** with the trend clear or accelerating, **momentum is typically to the downside for the general market.**
- **Trading Volume: Trading volume is an important indicator of market health**—light volume means trends may be transitory, strong volume is a confirming data point for a trend. There are several subsets of volume data:
  - One subset of volume data is the amount of shares, and options, purchased on the Ask versus the Bid. Volume buying on the Ask means people want the stock or the ETF and are in a hurry—they are not willing to wait for the price to come down to the Bid price. The inverse is less true but strong volume on the Bid indicates people wanting to sell rather than waiting for their Ask price. There are several data services that have this data.
  - Volume as measured by lower prices from the previous trade in the stock and volume as measured by higher prices from the previous trade. This is a daily statistic produced by all the exchanges. A trend of greater down rather than up volume is a clearly **bearish indicator.**

- **When the Financial Stocks are in a Bear Trend.** Historically the general market cannot move up without a positive trend coming out of financial stocks. You can track this easily by comparing the DJIA with the XLF and ETF of the financial sector. (See Figure 10.1.)
- **When the Dow Transports Confirm the DJIA:** Many professionals and traders still adhere to Dow Theory. A component of this approach to the market says that a bull market or rally is in place or coming when the Down Transportation Index moves up in tandem or ahead of the Dow Jones Industrial Average. I have seen the market move sharply upward as this nears and when it happens—investors planning to short the market need to be aware of this possibility.
- **When You Have a Hunch.** Once in a while the most experienced trader may quickly review a chart and pull the trigger on a trade. I am not that good and you should not assume you are either.
- **When You Think All Markets Are the Same:** The S&P 500, the Dow, and the NASDAQ 100 are different and do not assume they are equally valid places to short the market in general. The Dow and the S&P 500 trade closely, but the NASDAQ 100, without financial stocks, often diverges, so if you believe financials will play a big role in pulling the market lower, shorting the NASDAQ is not the way to go.

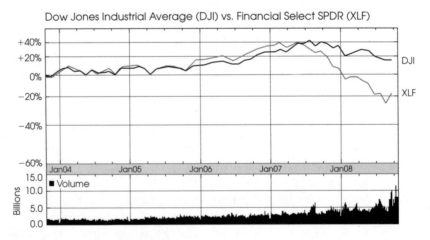

Figure 10.1   The DJIA and Financial Stocks

Source: CSI Data

How to Go Short

There are a myriad number of ways to short the general markets—I am going to keep it simple because those are invariably the easiest to get into and the easiest to manage. But before you begin, remember, you are not a trader and this is not a book about trading strategies. This is about using trading tools to short stocks, segments, and markets based on fundamentals—not active trading in and out of positions on a day-to-day basis.

Shorting general markets is highly similar to shorting market segments and much of the following material is a bit repetitive. In this section I make specific recommendations on what index options and ETFs to use; their liquidity and other characteristics should not change measurably in the coming months.

- **Puts on Indexes:** Index options are tied directly to an index. They are not tied to a basket of stocks; rather they are tied to an underlying dollar value that is the equivalent of the index level multiplied by some dollar amount, in the case of the S&P 500 index options, $100. These puts are highly efficient, low-cost trading tools that change hands in the millions each day. They trade like regular options.
- **Puts on Long ETFs:** As with market segments, this is a straightforward way to short a market index. The ETF is based on an underlying basket of stocks that mirror the index in question.
- **Short ETFs:** These ETFs perform in a manner inverse to the index—for every dollar the S&P goes down, a short ETF for the S&P 500 will go up one dollar. There are also double-short ETFs—for every dollar the index goes down, the ETFs go up roughly two dollars.
- **Calls on Short ETFs:** These are rocket-fueled trading tools to play the market's direction. For example, on a day the S&P 500 is down 0.62 percent, the double ETF (the SDS) is up 1.8 percent and the closest in calls—the August $65—are up 40 percent. Gotta love leverage, and as I wrote before, this can also work against you.
- **Selling Puts on Short ETFs:** A slightly more conservative way to get even more leverage on double short and single-short ETFs—is to sell puts.

As I wrote in the market segment section, when you sell a put you are selling someone the right to "put" the stock or ETF to you at a given price. For example, the SDS, the double-short ETF on the S&P 500, is now at $65 and change. You sell a September $63 put, collecting $300 per contract, because you think the price of the market is going down and the price of the SDS is going to rise. If in September the price of the ETF is above $63, the put will expire worthless—you have no obligation to buy the ETF itself.

This is a trade to make when you are convinced the longer term trend is in your favor—in this case, if you were a secular bear or simply do not think there is a sustainable rally on the horizon. There are some limitations. For example, most brokers require you have enough cash in an account to cover the cost of the ETFs or stocks if they are put to you.

Creating These Positions

I have prepared a brief list of the most liquid and efficient tools for trading the S&P, the Dow, and the NASDAQ just to get you started. I have not put in anything on the NASDAQ Composite—I would start (and stick with) this NASDAQ 100 as these largest 100 stocks drive the composite index as it is weighted by market cap.

The S&P 500

- For index option puts, the SPX
- For short ETFs, the Short S&P500 ProShares (SH)
- For double-short ETFs, the UltraShort S&P 500 ProShares (SDS)

The NASDAQ 100

- For index options, the NDX
- For long ETFs, the PowerShares QQQ (symbol QQQQ)
- For short ETFs, the Short QQQ ProShares (PSQ)
- For double-short ETFs, the Powershares Ultrashort QQQ (QID)

The Dow

- For index options, the DJX
- For long ETFs, the Diamond Trust Series 1 (DIA)

- For short ETFs, Short Dow30 ProShares (DOG)—*best symbol in the market but not very liquid*
- For double-short ETFs, UltraShort Dow30 ProShares (DXD)

A complete list can be found at any one of a number of sites. I would start at ETF Central on Yahoo.

Sample Trades

Here are a couple of sample trades, one built around a binary event—the earnings of financial institutions—the other part of a strategy for a secular bear market.

Trade #1—Financial Bad News

You are anticipating bad earnings news from financial stocks that will take the market down, at least for a while, and you buy puts on the ETF for the S&P 500 (SPX), the index that is more heavily weighted toward financials than the Dow. The earnings will be coming out in six weeks and you buy puts two months out and, as always, you are looking for a double. The SPX is currently at 129, typically at roughly one-tenth the value of the S&P, which is at 1285; what put should you buy? The same rules apply as you used to buy a put on a stock.

- **Setting a target price:** First you need to set a target for the index, the S&P 500. Take a look at the most recent low—in the past six months to a year, it should pop out of a chart—and it is the low just before the Treasury bailout of Freddie Mac and Fannie Mae and the enforcement of prohibitions against naked shorting of financial stocks were announced by the SEC. That low is 1215. You set two potential target prices: You look at puts on the S&P if it hits 1215 and if it goes halfway to its low, a rule of thumb I use when setting target prices.
- **Put pricing:** Since you divide by 10, you are looking at the $122 and the $125 puts on the SPY. The $122 are $2.42; the $125, $3.35. They are both out of the money so all you have is time value and that part of the put premium created by volatility and the desire of people to own these puts. Using simple math, assume half this premium will

wear off in the first month, the rest in the second month if the S&P stays static.

- **Which Put?:** You are making this trade because you think you are right and so you assume the S&P will retest the old lows after the last of the banks' earnings are announced in October—aware that several big banks announce in September. You make a simple assumption: the S&P could fall halfway to the previous low in the next month. Where will the two puts end up?

    The $122, priced at $2.42 loses $1.21 in premium due to time decay. It gains $3.00 due to the fall of the S&P to 12,550 and the SPX is at $125.50—I am keeping everything else static as volatility will be increasing and leverage decreasing at the same time—and the puts are now trading at $4.21. The $125 put has lost $0.25 due to time decay and is now almost in the money. It too has added three and a half points and is now worth $6.70. It has doubled—and the $122 put is not far behind.

    Which one do you buy? You go for the double—you have to assume your assumptions are correct—and buy the $125 put.

    As I wrote in previous chapters, this is a crude analysis I have created for the purposes of illustrating a point: Go for the first double.

Trade #2—The Secular Bear Market

How would you short a secular bear market? Let me count the ways—short the Dow, it has declined the most in most recent bear downturns; short the S&P because it has more financial stocks and they seem to be in the most trouble; short the NASDAQ because these growth stocks have the highest earnings multiples and are most exposed to a contraction in earnings, especially from overseas, where you see a slowdown and the inevitable rise in the greenback.

Aha! There is a nontechnical reason you think we are in a bear market. And that is the key. If you make a macro call about the market, up or down, examine what is behind the call and choose what you will short accordingly.

- **Set a Target Price:** You can perform all the analyses in the world but **predicting the exact duration and intensity of a**

fall in a market is a black art. You know this and just want to invest in a long-term secular trend, so what to do? You opt for my six-month rule: Where should the NASDAQ be in six months? You will worry about the rest of the bear market after the six months are up.

Assume the NASDAQ is 2420 and has held up well compared to the other indices. The P/E is 20—much higher than the S&P or Dow, in part because investors are also paying for growth. But growth is slowing down, and you go back to my rules, you short a company when the financial metric that made the stock run changes course. The issue for NASDAQ stocks is growth, not profits, and you see growth diminishing almost everywhere in the fourth quarter. The instrument you will short is the QQQ, the ETF that tracks the NASDAQ 100 and is currently at 47.70. The low in the last six months is just a smidge above $41.20. That is your target for six months: the previous six-month low.

- **ETF Pricing:** Your original thoughts were to buy a double-short ETF—you look at the chart and see the QID, the double-short ETF has not tracked the QQQ—the NASDAQ 100—very well in the past few months. You turn to the PSQ, the single-short ETF and it clearly tracks the QQQ well and you opt to use this to short the NASDAQ.

This is a simple trade. With the NASDAQ at 2420 and the QQQs at $47.70, this ETF is at $55.58. If the QQQs hit the target of $41.70, the ETF will hit (roughly) $61 to $62, a 10 percent gain in three to six months, a modest and low-risk way to short any index.

Conclusion

Shorting indices has a great deal of profit potential and can also be used to hedge parts of your portfolio, but this is also the beginning of a slippery slope into trading the markets and that is a game for professional or full-time traders. You have been warned.

Playing slides in market indices can be very profitable and there are a large number of trading instruments at your disposal to do so. The trick, problem, issue—whatever you want to call it—is the age-old challenge of timing the market. Successfully timing the market is difficult to do, but if you see fundamental problems and believe the market is going down, longer term put positions can work. If you want to play the market with some regularity, to trade it rather than make one investment or trade based on fundamentals, you will need to study up on advanced trading techniques to minimize your risk and preserve capital—something beyond the scope of this book.

Q&A

Q1. You make this sound so simple. Is it this simple when the market is melting down or running up and you are trying to get into a position?

We are many chapters into this book and I assume you have read the build up to where we are right now. That said, it is pretty simple— but your question implies you have tried to do this before and found yourself chasing a specific put. Yes, you need to set targets, and put your order in, and if the trade does not go off, it does not go off. The same discipline you need with any trade. And if you are a secular bear, moving the trade to a put with a much likelier chance to be purchased is no big deal.

Q2. The SPX is an ETF?

Nope. It is a financial instrument that represents the S&P 500 but is not an ETF. If you are playing the downside, puts on the SPX are the most widely traded options—put options—in the world.

Q3. Hedging—can you explain more about hedging your portfolio?

Let's say you are long—as most of us are—with the larger part of your portfolio. You do not want to move in and out of positions—you have a full-time job and no taste for doing this—but you fear a sharp market correction and see no need to suffer through it without protecting your existing long position or perhaps making a couple of bucks due to the correction.

You have $250,000 in the market and you fear a correction would take this value down to $200,000. You could do several things:

- buy puts on the S&P 500 (the SPX) that will produce a $50,000 gain if the market, as represented by the S&P 500 index, goes down 20 percent
- sell calls on the individual positions in your portfolio and use the cash to pay for the puts on the SPX
- sell calls on the individual positions in your portfolio and buy puts on the individual positions in your portfolio

(Continued)

In my own portfolio, in the past, I have sold calls on some of my positions and used the cash to buy S&P puts—I have never tried to buy puts to cover 100 percent of my downside risk. What you do depends on how much you want to spend and how much upside you are willing to give up by selling calls on your existing positions.

Rules

- The S&P 500 is considered—and is—more representative of corporate and economic performance than the Dow.
- You should invest against the market if you see a downturn coming and not try to day-trade market indexes.
- Simplicity is the key to success—you should master one or just a few methods to play market movements.
- The NASDAQ 100 is the index traders short when betting against technology companies as a whole.
- If you want to short the market do not do it when the 50-day moving average is moving up strongly.
- If there is a steady trend showing new lows outpacing new highs, momentum is typically to the downside for the general market.
- Do not short when the Dow Transports confirm the DJIA.
- Do not short when you have a hunch.
- Do not assume all markets are the same.
- Predicting the exact duration and intensity of a fall in a market is a black art.

11

Managing a Position or Everyone Has a Plan Until They Get Punched in the Face

The easy part is over—now you have your money in hand, you are about to buy puts or buy calls on a short ETF or you may even be ready to short a stock. Now the emotional side comes into play, and managing this is much harder than all the research, analysis, and thinking you have done to date. Yes, you are a successful investor, even familiar with calls and puts, but you have never held a long-term put position through a market rally.

But you have a plan you say? To quote that famous investor (and ear-biter) Mike Tyson, **"Everyone has a plan until they get punched in the face."** This chapter is about managing through the first and subsequent punches you will eventually absorb when managing longer term put positions.

My service typically has 30 or more open positions and I take the responsibility of managing these positions for subscribers, keeping them informed of developments, closing positions, or changing recommended Buy Under prices. It is much harder than deciding to open a position—there are many more variables involved, including greed and fear.

Personal Management Rules

What I am about to write you have read or should have read before— no matter, read it again. I remember when I was a regional sales manager for AT&T I complained when I was pulled out of the field for routine sales training. I was going to learn nothing new, I said. And I did not, but I sure got a chance to remember a good deal I had forgotten in the day-to-day managing of accounts and employees. The same is true for managing positions.

- Check your ego at the door.
- Check your emotions, when possible, at the door.
- Wait for the great trade—do not force a trade.
- Positions are inanimate objects—they deserve no affection or love from you.
- Volatility is not risk. Repeat after me, volatility is not risk.
- Admitting mistakes is harder than fixing them.
- If you make a mistake, respond immediately.
- No one ever lost money by taking profits.

I know you have heard them before—so have I and I think about them every time I ignore them and lose money.

Remembering the Position Management Rules and the Basics

Before we delve into the basics of managing a position, a little refresher here is necessary. You know most of this, but it never hurts to review and remind yourself of the obvious because more often than not the obvious works and works well. It is important that you remember these position management rules:

- Play great defense; be opportunistic on offense when making a trade.
- Take more risks with profits than with initial capital.
- Take one approach to shorting—learn it well.
- It's all cash at 4 P.M.—view every position as the equivalent of cash.
- Your entry point is yesterday's close—it's not what you paid, it's what the position is worth.
- Volatility is not risk. Repeat after me, volatility is not risk.
- Add capital to successful positions.
- If the story changes, and you cannot see the stock hitting its target price, close the position. Repeat after me, if the stock cannot hit the target price, run like hell.

To borrow a phrase from the Centers for Disease Control and bad television detective shows, "when you hear hoof beats, don't think zebras." Translation: go with the basics first, place and manage your trades in a manner that first makes great sense.

- **Playing Defense: The heart of virtually all successful investing, and trading, is playing defense**—avoiding mistakes and preserving capital. And what I believe in is preserving capital and swinging for home runs. The more capital you have, the more swings you have for hitting home runs.
- **Hitting Home Runs:** If you want to earn 5 percent, buy a bond. If you want aggressive growth, read my biotech blog. This is about hitting home runs with your high risk capital. **The initial target for every position should be a double—a 100 percent gain.**
- **Press When You Can: To hit home runs you have to press your profits**—preserve initial capital at all costs but you should press with some of your profits. Consider adding capital if a position is working well but never let one position be overweight more than 10 percent of your risk capital and only when the position is working.
- **Be Consistent: Take one approach and make it work. Get a structure that works and stick to it.** The best analogy is from the real world—one of my sons has a natural and occasionally wonderful left-handed swing as a baseball player. Multiple coaches managed to ruin it over a two-year period. Then his high school coach gave him clear guidance to hit for power and to perfect this skill he has worked with one coach, one set of rules, one structure all summer. The first bomb was hit after three months of instruction from the same coach—it takes time to master a new stroke—and to master a new kind of investing.
- **When the Story Changes: When the rationale for buying into a position changes, cut and run.**
- **Forget History: Never worry about what you put into a position; worry about what you can get out,** what is done is done, what has been spent has been spent.
- **Volatility is Not Risk: Puts can lose a lot of value in a short period of time. This is volatility, not risk.** I recommended buying puts on EMC that lost 85 percent of their value in three

months. I saw data telling me their subsidiary VMWare was going to have less than a gangbuster quarter. VMWare missed and a day later the EMC position was up more than 25 percent—the temporary fall in the put was nerve wracking but incidental as I believed in the underlying problems with VMWare's fundamentals.

Managing an Open Position

This is the fun part. And it's the hardest part if you are not using hard price targets and sell stops, which we are not. Did I mention that? Many successful investors, including successful options traders I know, set hard price targets and stop losses. This means if a put hits a target price or comes down and hits a certain price you are out of the position. This discipline is at the heart of successful technical trading, and it would kill many great short positions. I am recommending you hold put positions for longer periods of time than technical traders do and with this approach you have to ride out volatility and big swings in the put price.

There are some things to do other than the obvious of tracking the price of the put you bought, and you need to do these to optimize profits and minimize losses.

- **Track the Underlying Stock:** Sounds dumb but many people forget to track the individual stock. Keep an eye on it. If technical indicators such as the 50-day moving average are violated—the stock breaks through and stays there—you may want to close the position if you are within two months of expiration.
- **Track Premiums:** What I mean here is to **track the relationship of the price of the put to the price of the stock.** Even if you have an out-of-the-money put, it is best to do this with an in-the-money put. For example, Sunset Biotech is trading at $23 in May and a $25 July put is trading for $3.50. It is $2 in the money so the premium on the put is $1.50 for about two months. If this premium is exactly the same—the put still trades for $3.50 and the stock is $23 a month later—then sentiment is bearish. I recommend looking at this because it is a much faster and simpler way

to measure sentiment than all the analytical nonsense you can read in a book.

- **Track the Put/Call Ratio:** This takes more work—I have one of my sons do it when he remembers to—you are simply tracking the ratio of puts to calls. What you want to see is if this ratio is headed your way—more and more puts—although this increased liquidity may actually serve to reduce the premium on your puts as they are more readily available.

- **Track Variations in Put Prices:** Puts are available for several or many months on a given stock, index, or ETF. In theory, they should all be priced the same with variations based on the decay of the value of the put over time. But this rarely happens and occasionally there is a large discontinuity in the price and/or the volume of puts month to month. And this is a sign traders believe something is going to happen, good or bad, with the company and the underlying stock in a given period of time.

  For example, Apple began to trade up in anticipation of the shipping date of the new 3G version of the iPhone. Put activity increased as traders—some traders—believed Apple would miss the shipment date. There was an increasingly heavy concentration of put buying the month the new phone was to ship. What was interesting was the number of calls being purchased also increased dramatically.

  What should you look for as an indicator of market sentiment and perhaps an opportunity to close out a trade ahead of an announcement? Look for a month with heavy buying in puts that is not matched by heavy buying of calls.

- **Track Collateral Positions:** Sometimes the logic of a deteriorating market segment is so compelling you may find yourself with a concentration of positions directly related to each other—in the short or long term—that can be harmful if a market segment moves against you. Even I, Grand Poobah of shorting that I am, found myself with too many open recommendations in the financial and homebuilding sector as they traded alongside each other in January 2008, and watched as the stocks bounced up based on false optimism and short covering.

Managing through Catalysts

Catalysts can be a good thing—earnings are unexpectedly way down, wahoo!—or a bad thing—some company thinks they can turn straw into gold and buys a 20 percent stake in a dying company you have shorted. Getting through catalysts can be harder than predicting them.

- **Define Upcoming Catalysts:** No, you don't have to write a report, **just keep a list in your head** or on the scraps of paper I use to make a brief list of catalysts that can upset my positions, from earnings to a Fed decision on interest rates. If they are repeated events like earnings, check to see how the stock moved around the last couple of earnings announcements, or the last time the Fed raised rates, and so on. You will quickly see what is important and what is not.
- **Define a Trading Range: Try to figure out what the trading range on the stock might be, up or down, once this catalyst occurs.** Then try to do the same for your put. This is not that hard: Just eyeball it, forget the calculator. If this target range brings your put into home run territory—a 100 percent gain, a double, or even near it—you need to start thinking about getting out or rolling the position into a different put (keep reading, rolling is in this chapter.)
- **Set a Stop Loss: Stop losses rarely work when trading volatile stocks and options**—you invariably get stopped out and then the position moves in your direction. That being said, I do see a value in trailing stop losses for profitable positions. For example, you bought a Pfizer $20 put at $1.20 and the stock is $17—I would have rolled the position, more on that in a minute—and it is now worth $3.35, a big, big winner. You might set a stop loss of $3 or $2.50 or what have you—your call—as their earnings announcements are coming up and the stock could move against you. There is nothing wrong with taking profits, even if you take them early.

  Setting a stop loss for a position is one way to protect yourself against the story changing. **But I do not recommend them for most positions as puts are too volatile.** I could give you many examples from my own portfolio or from my service but I believe the way to manage risk is to manage the amount of capital you allocate to a trade, take profits, and accept losses in a disciplined way and stick with fundamentals.

Rolling and Pressing a Position

The ability to roll or press a position—or do both—is, without a doubt, the single greatest advantage put buyers have when shorting a stock compared to borrowing shares and shorting the company the traditional way.

Rolling a Position

A trader who rolls a position closes a successful position—never a losing one, repeat after me, never a losing one—and buys another put at a lower strike price and/or a later date. You do this when the fundamental thesis about the underlying company and stock is still in place and technical indicators are in your favor. Simply put, **you roll into a new put using the same discipline and selection method as if it were a wholly new position.**

When you do this, you have a few alternatives:

- Take all the dough, including profits, and buy the new put. In this case you are **rolling and pressing.**
- **Take your profits off the table** and invest your original capital in the new position. This is rolling.
- **Change the size of the new position** based on your current management of your portfolio.

In the fall of 2007 lots of data points were flashing a warning—consumer spending was slowing or would slow soon. History tells us one of the first victims during a spending slowdown is women's clothing—for many a discretionary purchase—and I went trolling around looking for a good short, no, a great short position. Using tools available to you—public information available through Yahoo—I found a company struggling and going through management turmoil even when consumer spending was robust: Liz Claiborne. The company had incredible exposure to the women's clothing market with brands that were already failing in the marketplace. LIZ also faced many potential negative catalysts for it was struggling to sell some brands to other outfits—but who buys struggling brands when demand is pulling back? On September 27,

2007, long before holiday sales data was in from other sources, I recommended buying the January 30 puts—these closed out with a gain of 163 percent and I recommended subscribers buy the January 25 puts. These produced a gain of 169 percent and I kept it going—I recommended the April $22.50 puts, closed the position on January 10 with a gain of 156 percent, bought new July $15 puts at $1.20 and closed them out at $3.60 in July, plus 200 percent. The total gain on this play on consumer discretionary spending returned 689 percent while the sector itself, as measured by the ETF known as the XLY, was down just 11 percent at the same time. A great, great trade the perfect **marriage of a bad company in a sliding** segment. (See Figure 11.1.)

How exactly does this work?

When you roll a position and use the captured profits, you need to do a couple of things:

- Make sure it is not more than double the size of the maximum position you allow within your portfolio or 10 percent, whichever is lower.
- Put in trailing stop losses set to ensure you keep some percentage of your profits. The best way to do this is to have a stop loss for a percentage of the new puts, not the whole position. For example, if the initial position doubled, and you pressed all of this into a new position, you could set up a stop loss that would ensure you keep a 50 percent profit or one

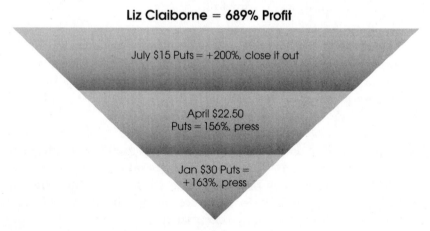

Liz Claiborne = 689% Profit

July $15 Puts = +200%, close it out

April $22.50
Puts = 156%, press

Jan $30 Puts =
+163%, press

Figure 11.1   LIZ

that kicks in when the new put has lost its worth or 75 percent of your purchase price.

Pressing a Position

This is a fancy term for putting more money to work—either when you roll a position and put some or all of your profits into this new put or when you simply double up and put more money to work on a winning position.

When should you press?

- The fundamental lousy company story has not changed.
- Technical indicators are all flashing green: The stock is falling and below its 50-day and 200-day moving averages, volume is increasing as the stock price falls, the put/call ratio is increasing in favor of puts.
- When a position is up at least 40 percent and has been above that level for a considerable period of time—at least two weeks, preferably more.
- When there are at least two months to expiration.

You do not press under the following conditions:

- When a position is underwater—this is not blackjack—**you never, ever press on a losing position.** For example, the last time I recommended shorting Amgen with puts, the positions moved against me almost immediately. The stock was in the low $40s and I saw $35 on the horizon after having rolled puts a couple of times on Amgen from an initial starting point in the mid $50s. I was tempted to send out an alert and tell people to double up—and resisted the urge. I resisted the urge at $45, $48, $50, $55, and eventually closed the position at a near total loss, although the total investment in Amgen was a big winner. If I had doubled up—bought more puts as they fell in price—the losses on this last put position would have wiped out all the gains from the previous positions.
- **You never put more than twice your normal portfolio allocation**—or 10 percent, whichever is less—into one position.
- **Do not close a position to ride another one unless you would have closed that position anyway.** Use extra cash. If you don't

have any extra cash, wait until you should close another position before pressing.

- **You play a hunch**—man, my winner is winning and I want it to win some more—take it from a Mets fan from the 1960s—winning can be temporary, hunches don't work in the long run.

A Momentum Approach

Everyone manages their own portfolios differently—and portfolio management intersects directly with how you roll and press positions. I met someone recently at a Money Show, a trade show for individual investors, who told me about a neat but high-risk capital allocation system well suited to rolling and pressing positions. In this person's portfolio management system you put 3.5 percent (or some other percentage) of your high risk or trading capital into any put position—and you assume you are smart and keep an extra 3.5 percent in reserve for any position. If a position works well quickly you do one of two things:

1. You press and pour it on and use sell stops to make sure you never ever lose any original capital.
2. You roll the position to the next strike price in the same month *and* press at the same time. You set sell stops to protect your original capital.

This approach is clearly designed to take advantage of downside momentum in a relatively fast-moving stock. And it also requires a fairly high level of scrutiny and position management on a day-to-day basis. And it is high risk—sell stops can quickly take you out of positions you do not want to leave. That said, I get enough e-mail about trading momentum I thought I would offer it up as a simple way to make—or lose money, profits actually—on one trading position.

Getting Out

A more polished writer would call this "Exit Strategies." Well, you and I know, and every trader knows, the proper expression, often spoken at the top of one's lungs to a broker on the other end of the phone is "get out."

There is only so much one can write about "getting out"—so much has to do with an individual's portfolio, their ability to manage volatility, and to manage risk, and the possibility of moving money to other opportunities and positions. Being the brave, decisive soul that I am, I recommend you look at a few approaches outlined below.

One additional note about getting out—what to do in the face of an old-fashioned bull rally with legs. In late 2008, the Obama rally hit many of my put positions hard, but I saw this as a temporal rally, nothing with legs. Fortunately, I was quite right. If you see a bull rally moving all stocks upward, good and bad, and if you think it has legs of three to six months or more, consider closing all your positions out.

It's Cash at 4 P.M.

My first stock broker, the aforementioned Rodney Madrid, used to convince me to close a position by saying **"it's all cash at 4 P.M."** And he was right. He would also occasionally scream "You can buy groceries with it," when I was not listening to him. In 1987, before online trading and 24/7 coverage of news, I read a one-paragraph mention of a special analysts meeting being held in two-and-a-half weeks by the Lotus Development Corporation, the maker of Lotus 1-2-3, the market-leading spreadsheet before Excel conquered the world. I figured companies did not hold special meetings to announce bad news—at least not then. I called Rodney. The stock was trading around $27 (these are approximations, it was a long time ago) and the $30 call option was trading at $0.50. I took a big chunk of my available trading cash—I had a tiny portfolio with one stock and an upcoming purchase of a house—and bought 100 contracts. Of course, the stock went down to $24. I doubled up and bought another 100 contracts at $0.25.

Five days before expiration of the calls Lotus held the special analysts meeting and announced a 10-year development agreement with IBM. The stock rocketed to around $33. You could hear Rodney screaming without the use of the telephone even though he was 30 miles away—"get out, get out." I did. I had made a year's salary, walked out of my office, threw up in a bush (I was not in this industry, this was an amateur doubling his salary) on the way to the parking lot, and went home for the day. The stock did go higher. It touched 37 if I remember correctly, so I left another year's salary on the table, but I could have cared less.

Don't be confused. I am not suggesting you close all positions before the close, but **viewing your short positions as being perfectly liquid pushes you to evaluate them,** not to sit on them.

The Targets Have Not Been Met

My method is based on fundamentals—yours should be too—and that means you need to evaluate how your positions are performing relative to your expectations, based on fundamentals, with some side glances at technical indicators. You should have target prices for underlying stocks based on fundamentals and the company story. If these change—specifically fundamentals—then you may change the target prices for the underlying stock and when that happens you need to reevaluate the puts and perhaps get out. The bottom line: Stick with original targets for the underlying stock, and the 100 percent rule for potential profits on the map until—until it is no longer time to do so.

Be flexible. How flexible? Not too flexible. Consider some of the following guidelines when managing your positions.

- **If you are at or near your 100 percent gain,** you must consider closing the position. You may still see the fundamentals of the company weakening and you may create a new position but this is not automatic either.
- **If an out-of-the-money put is less than one month from expiration,** and there are no upcoming catalysts, and the put is out of the money by more dollars than the stock has moved up or down in the past month, you are probably not going to hit your target and it could be time to get out. For example, let's say the Shulman Regional Bank has already announced earnings, they were in line, the stock is holding up at $24, you own $17.50 puts, and even with the volatility of the financial sector the stock has traded no more than $4.50—from $19.50 to $24—in the past month and a half. It is highly unlikely it is going to come down to your target, so it is time

to take your losses and move on. The contrary example is the one of EMC I wrote about earlier. I waited because I knew a catalyst was coming and the stock could still move dramatically.

- **If the underlying stock has broken above its 50-day moving average,** and continues to move up on increasing volume, this is a good time to move out of any position but especially one with no catalysts and an expiration date within 90 days. One caveat—check the number of shares held short to see if this movement is being driven by short covering. If you believe it is, and the fundamental story is the same, give the position more time.

When Stories Change

When the company story changes, you need to reassess, and if it is a change that fundamentally alters the prospects for the company, get out. No doubt you may give up future profits and take losses if you follow this, but you must— if you based your short positions on fundamentals, you need to close them when these fundamentals change against you. I had a great success recommending short positions in the deep discounters—Dollar Tree and Tuesday Morning—since the folks on the lowest end of the consumer totem pole were going to be hit first and hardest by a recession. Then, Congress began to debate a bill to give $150 billion in rebates to people—and the customers of these two chains were most likely to take that rebate and spend it at a discount store. As passage of the bill became ever more likely, I closed the positions.

The Tides Begin to Turn—The Technicals Change

Sometimes technical indicators turn sharply against you and you should close a position if this happens and you are too close to expiration. For example, if a stock breaks through its 50-day moving average, stays there, or climbs, and there are no potential downside catalysts in sight, get ready to get out if the put is expiring in one to two months depending on how far the put is out of the money. If your target price for the stock has been pushed out of sight by a technical rally, it may be time to move on.

The Irrational or Cult Stock

Most stocks do not behave the way they should. And some stocks, I call them cult stocks, really don't behave the way they should. I have recommended shorting several of these—including Affymetrix and Palm—and while some positions made money, they were, for the most part, losing positions due to a high level of irrationality surrounding the cult stocks. These are hard to identify, but there are several common denominators:

- **They are former high fliers**, many in the technology sector.
- **They often are former purveyors of hot products** and have household names (Vonage and Palm come to mind).
- **They have a large component of retail investors**—you and me.

When Not to Get Out

There are times when every muscle in your body and the one in between you ears are screaming "get out, get out." The advice I am giving here is not related to managing your overall portfolio—sometimes you have to liquidate positions because of rules you have for managing your portfolio or you cannot resist and you have to buy that Bristol Blenheim. The following is guidance about managing an individual position **independent of portfolio considerations and market conditions.**

That being said, the **great villain**—the great driver of blood pressure and early exits—from otherwise winning positions **is volatility.** I must say this at least once a day in conversation, e-mail, or in seminars: "volatility is not risk." When a position or your portfolio is getting whacked by short-term volatility, it is sometimes hard to make the distinction. But you must. If you cannot, stay long.

What kinds of volatility can you expect to experience and you should learn to weather or, sometimes, interpret as a sign to close a position?

- **The One Day, One-Off Disruption:** We have all been through this on the long side as well—something happens that completely turns your stomach and puts your position underwater. It could be Goldman Sachs putting a company you have shorted on the Conviction Buy List; a new government program; and so on. When this happens go to work—read all you can—and then watch the stock for a few days and see if the one-day rally gathers strength. The hard part will be to separate real buying from short covering (see below). This all sounds obvious but if you look at charts, stocks will often pop up, momentum traders get in, the stock drops a bit, and then will either renew a slide or start climbing. This can take days, not hours, to play out.

- **Short Covering and Short Squeezes:** These technical rallies are the bane of nervous short-side investors and the biggest driver of sales of blood pressure monitoring equipment in recent years. And they are just that—short-term technical rallies with no ongoing support from serious investors. Some last a day—some several days—and they are characterized by above-average daily trading volumes and declines in short positions. Unfortunately, the services that track daily changes in short positions are somewhat expensive—$600 and up at last glance—but you will be able to get a sense of what is going on by reading and trolling the Web. Another clue that a rally is short covering: The puts do not decline in value nearly as much as you would expect, especially those at least two months from expiration.

  A good example of the yo-yo stock driven by short covering is First Fed Financial, a regional bank with oodles of issues in the middle of 2008. A short position—puts—in the stock was doing incredibly well when that July Sir Hank Paulson, the white knight of irresponsible banks and millionaire CEOs, spoke and said this and that and then extended a lifeline to Fannie and Freddie. Short sellers covered, the stock bounced more, the shorts covered again and the $3 to $4 stock quickly moved to $12. The put was several months out and eventually worked, but these kinds of spikes, which occurred several times with the Fed, were truly nerve wracking.

- **A Technical Bounce:** At times a stock or market segment will be oversold—the word means what it says, the stock or segment has been sold off so hard that short-term traders pile in expecting a bounce. These situations are easy to spot: a sharp reversal of downside volume and a spike in the price, and these technical rallies typically end in five days or less for a stock, 10 days or less for a market segment, and come to screeching halt when the stock or an ETF representing a segment hits a 50-day moving average.

- **An Exogenous Event:** Sometimes, ah, stuff happens. From 9/11 to the Bear Stearns meltdown to Eddie Lambert buying Sears, there are events that mess up your position in a company. There is nothing you can do about it—but you must take a hard look at the put position you have in place and see if this event has fundamentally changed the valuation the market has put on your company and segment and whether Street expectations have changed so dramatically your position cannot recover before expiration. Admittedly, this is difficult to do. And if you find yourself at a loss, unable to determine the impact of the event on your position, go back to a previously discussed rule or approach—it is all cash at 4 P.M.—liquidate the position. There is always another great trade waiting for the patient trader.

When Volatility Is Risk

There are times volatility actually is risk—and this is easy to miss if you really believe you have a great position, a great trade in place. When does volatility become risk?

- **When short term volatility** moves a position so much there is little chance to recover before expiration.
- **When a technical or event-driven bounce** pushes a stock above a critical moving average—typically the 50-day moving average—and the stock stays there too long. This means technical-based trading has pushed a stock into a zone where other investors may be piling in and the upside momentum is too much to withstand. This caution applies only when that stock has not been pushed by a major market rally and has moved up way ahead of the action in the general market.
- When volatility means the **underlying fundamentals of the company or Street expectations are changing** and you—and I—are missing this change. For example, I recommended shorting Amgen in the mid $50s, near $60 and the stock fell steadily toward $40. I rolled the position a couple of times and felt the stock should bottom around $35. But it bounced and bounced between $40 and $45 and then took off. After the stock stayed above $45 for a couple of weeks money poured in—as it did into other large-cap biotechs—and the trade was effectively blown up.

Managing Multiple Positions

Sometimes all hell breaks loose and everything you own, long or short, goes against you. You have 1 or 10 or 30 positions and they are all showing red. What to do?

- **Stay calm:** I know, easier said than done, and that is a topic of several hundred noninvestment books written across time.
- **Assess and manage each position as a stand-alone position**—one at a time, independent of the market—which they should be except for a major, gigantic bull rally.
- **Take solace in history and a look at former rallies:** I was speaking about shorting at a Money Show a day after the Dow Jones Industrial Average staged a 300-point rally. Oops. Yet my session was fully attended, people were calm, and most asked questions about individual positions. Why? They knew, as I did, that of the twenty 300- (or more) point rallies in the Dow, every one took place in a bear market.

Truly the critical thing for you to do is to **evaluate each position individually** and close those with profit potential that has changed due to changes in the technical standing of the market.

For instance, you may be managing multiple positions that are related—investment banks and regional banks, banks and home builders, retail and travel, and so on. There are times when these positions will move in tandem and torture you. This is the time to measure these interdependencies and make changes if necessary to avoid exposure to a market move that hits too many of your positions. It is very tempting to pile onto one great trade. For example, in 2007 the home builders were the equivalent of shooting fish in a barrel, in 2008 the financials were like shooting fish with a cruise missile in a barrel, but these guys did bounce around and in January and July 2008; the positions in both sectors were temporarily whacked by technical trading and exogenous events. I looked at my list of recommendations and realized a subscriber who was buying every recommendation was over-exposed to these short-term (and eventually meaningless) gyrations. Let me reiterate—**do not expose yourself to any one position (even a position you press or roll) with more than 10 percent of your portfolio** and I would not go above 20 percent for collateral positions.

Conclusion

Managing a position is much harder than getting into one, at least for this fella. Since you have already fallen in love with the trade—that is why you put it on—you have put your money where your brain and heart are and you can count the money you are going to make when you are proven right.

And this is your greatest danger, so rather than recap everything, the advice here is simple: Be disciplined, through volatility, through taking profits, and through taking losses. Press your winners; stick to targets; manage to hit home runs—and if you find your discipline wavering or your thoughts about the potential for a position unclear due to changes in the market or the company, close the position.

Q&A

Q1. What is the most important thing to do when managing a position?

Never fall in love with your position, never accept that the underlying story might not change. Always review positions with a critical eye. Since my sons are readers of the draft, I cannot say "don't believe your own bull . . . t" but that sums it up best. This is true for underlying fundamentals, Wall Street expectations, and the technical indicators surrounding a position—the tripod we build underneath our selection of a company or segment or short.

Q2. If I agree with you, and I have 20 short positions out there, and the market hits me hard, and I am down 25 percent or more in my account, do I double up if I am convinced this is a short-term technical situation?

Every bone in my body wants to scream "go for it"—and I am a congenital optimist, I predicted the Giants would win the Super Bowl in 2008, I knew they would come back. But when it comes to investing, discipline must take over. So the unequivocal answer is no. You never double up or add any kind of money to a losing position for the simple reason you may be wrong. There is simply too much risk that you may be missing something, that short-term volatility may actually be a real, longer-term technical turn in your positions and your doubling up could turn your 25 percent loss into much more. For example, the Giants did win the Super Bowl but I have yet to collect on my bet with one of my sons—so I was right but so far the trade has not paid off.

(Continued)

Q3. What is the worst case of volatility you have been through that would help me stay calm?

A great question. Right after I rolled Citigroup in the second quarter of 2008—took profits, recommended a new put position with a lower strike price, I believe it was a $15 put—the stock broke back up and climbed above $20. And it appeared to be more than technical trading—it looked like real money flows from value investors, and in fact much of it was just that. Could not have been more than two or three days. And the entire sector moved up with the big C. I called hedge fund managers, trolled the Internet, and reread everything I had written about Citi and realized the only thing happening was sucker money was being pulled into the stock. The company still had hundreds of billions of dollars in questionable or hard-to-price off-balance-sheet assets, its core operating businesses were declining, and on its best day the stock was worth no more than $8 to $10 if that—my original target price for the stock. I kept my readers in the position and the stock eventually turned south again. The hard part was deciding that I knew more than all the folks investing as if Citi were at a bottom. As I write this, Citi sits at $2.90.

Rules

- The heart of virtually all successful investing, and trading, is playing defense.
- The initial target for every position should be a double—a 100 percent gain.
- To hit home runs you have to press your profits.
- Take one approach and make it work. Get a structure that works and stick to it.
- When the rationale for buying into a position changes, cut and run.
- Never worry about what you put into a position; worry about what you can get out.
- Puts can lose a lot of value in a short period of time. This is volatility, not risk.
- Track several things when managing a position: the price of the underlying stock; the relationship of the price of the put to the price of the stock; the put/call ratio; variations in put prices across different expiration dates; and always track collateral positions.
- Define a trading range for the stock.
- Make yourself aware of upcoming catalysts.
- Set trailing stop losses on profitable positions; do not set stop losses on other positions.
- View your short positions as being perfectly liquid each day.
- If you are at or near your 100 percent gain, you must consider closing the position.
- If an out-of-the-money put is less than one month from expiration, consider getting out.

(Continued)

- The ability to roll or press a position—or do both—is, without a doubt, the single greatest advantage put buyers have when shorting a stock compared to borrowing shares and shorting the company the traditional way.
- When you roll into a new put use the same discipline and selection method as if it were a wholly new position.
- When you roll a position and use the captured profits, you need to make sure it is not more than double the size of your maximum position and you put in trailing stop losses.
- You never, ever press on a losing position.
- Do not close a position to ride another one unless you would have closed that position anyway.
- Do not expose yourself to any one position (even a position you press or roll) with more than 10 percent of your portfolio.

CHAPTER

12

Shorting Commodities and Real Estate

In modern markets, you can short almost anything, including hard assets such as commodities and real estate. With the end of the real estate bubble and increasing interest in commodities, new financial instruments have been developed to make it easier for individual investors to short these assets.

Let's start with commodities.

Commodities Overview

Commodities ranging from oil to cotton historically have been shorted on commodity exchanges—and one trader once told me the one certainty is individuals playing commodities lose 100 percent of their capital 100 percent of the time. But times have changed. There are several ways, shown below, that individuals can short commodities with less risk than actually shorting futures contracts on those commodities. These ways are:

- **Buying puts on long ETFs** that are baskets of individual commodities or indices. These ETFs come in many different flavors ranging from tracking of indices and baskets of commodity contracts to ETFs that track movements in futures contracts.
- **Buying short and double-short ETFs** that track individual commodities or indices.
- **Buying puts on companies** that are pure plays on individual commodities, for example, ExxonMobil in the oil patch.

- **Buying puts on companies** that are suppliers to commodity producers (i.e., John Deere and agricultural commodities.).

The dynamics of commodity ETFs and equities are different from other equities in that they trade in a direct relationship with commodity prices—an external driver linked, in turn, to many factors not of primary importance when shorting other kinds of stocks and market segments. Translation: This is a different knowledge base and experience set. **Commodities, long term, trade on very core fundamentals**—supply and demand—far more than most stocks. In the short term they move based on many factors other than underlying fundamentals, far more than stocks do.

A note about these ETFs: Commodity ETFs attempt to mirror a commodity index or marketplace, but you need to look at their components and performance against the price of the underlying commodities. You can do all this on readily accessible websites such as Yahoo.

The prices of most commodities over the long term are set by supply and demand; in the short term they are set by a bunch of screaming traders plying their craft as commodity traders on exchanges such as the Chicago Mercantile Exchange. There are other materials and commodity exchanges around the world but a good deal happens in the pits in Chicago. More and more trading does take place computer to computer but there is still a wonderful amount of raw, capitalistic madness in evidence on the floor of the exchange. And this madness will drive your positions day to day. Be aware.

Oil and Gas

How to trade oil and gas to the downside? Let me count the ways.

1. **Buy puts on long ETFs:** There are many ETFs to choose from—my preference is for liquidity in both the ETFs and options. The best place to search is the Yahoo ETF Center where you can click on a header—Volume, 3 Month Avg, or IntradayVolume—and you can see what trades with the most liquidity.

- ◆ For oil, look at U.S. Oil (USO).
- ◆ For natural gas, look at Natural Gas (UNG).
- ◆ For the entire industry including equipment, exploration, and services companies, the Energy Select Sector SPDR (XLE).
2. **Buy double-short ETFs:** The most liquid double-short ETF is the UltraShort Oil & Gas ProShares (DUG).
3. **Buy puts on market leaders:** In oil and gas the stocks of companies in the business, such as ExxonMobil, are leading indicators of movements in pricing while ETFs are concomitant indicators—they move in tandem with commodity prices. Translation: If you feel oil is rising, is in a bubble that is still too hot to play by shorting based on the commodity price, you may want to buy a put on a market leader. Take a look at Figure 12.1, which shows a two-year chart for Exxon versus the ETF for oil.
4. **Buy puts on oil and gas services companies** (i.e., Haliburton).
5. **Buy puts on long ETFs in oil and gas services:** Another way to play a downturn in oil prices is to short the oil services and equipment industry. The dominant ETF here is the Services HOLDRS (OIH) that has liquid puts and tracks the general shape of the curve of oil prices.

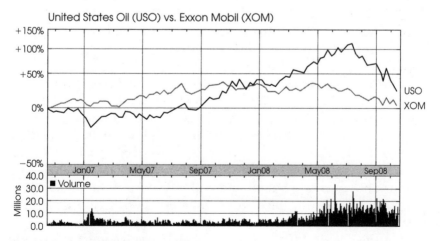

Figure 12.1   Exxon Two Year Chart vs. ETF for Oil

Source: CSI Data

What to choose? It depends on your time horizon.

- If you fear you are well ahead of a downturn but are convinced it is coming, short the market leaders—and in the oil market, they are easy to spot and easy to short.
- If you want to ride the oil price curve with moderate volatility, short the XLE.
- If you want to ride the oil price curve aggressively, buy the double-short ETF, the DUG.
- If you want to roll the dice, buy calls on the DUG. This is a high-risk, rocket-fueled trade that would have returned unspeakable amounts of money from July to August 2008 when oil fell from $147 to $103. This is a very high risk, so buyer beware, especially when geopolitics can blow you up.

This is enough to confuse any investor. If this is the sandbox you want to play in, I recommend you pick a set of tactics to implement your view oil of prices and master it. I would not dabble in all these tactics—find one method and make it work.

Basic Materials

This is going to sound a bit like a rerun of the oil and gas section so I will simply go right to my view: ETFs are the simplest instruments to use to short basic materials. Oh, what are basic materials? Seems like the names of funds and indices can be deceiving. Some indices include gold, others do not, some include chemicals, others exclude chemicals, and so on.

This means a great deal when you are processing information and deciding what you think of a market for a commodity and whether you want to short that market. For example, if you want iron ore to fall, these indices are probably too broad and you would have to short an iron ore producer. You also need to see what commodities move as a group—I am not a commodity expert—but I know enough that certain commodities move in tandem, others move alone, and you need to do your homework before taking a position.

For this reason I have listed several ETFs with some explanation of what they include in their market coverage.

Long ETFs (You Buy Puts on These)
This is a relatively short list—pardon the pun—as I prefer liquidity in puts.

- **Metals and Mining:** SPDR S&P Metals & Mining (XME). This ETF reflects precious metals such as gold, industrial metals including copper and aluminum, steel, and coal.
- **Broad Based Commodities:** PowerShares DB Commodity Index Tracking Fund (DBC). This ETF is based on an index that in turn is a metric for the following commodities: light sweet crude oil, heating oil, aluminum, gold, corn, and wheat. The weighting is based on historical levels of worldwide production.
- **Basic Commodities and Finished Materials:** Materials Select Sector SPDR (XLB). This ETF has holdings in chemicals, construction materials, containers and packaging, materials and mining, and paper and forest products.

Double-Short ETFs

- **Basic Commodities:** UltraShort Basic Materials ProShares (SMN). This ETF moves up, in theory, two dollars for every dollar the Dow Jones U.S. Basic Materials index goes down. That index is stock-based—it moves on stock prices, not on the prices of commodities—and covers virtually all basic materials including chemicals, paper, and precious metals.
- As you can see there are major differences among these ETFs and what they try to reflect in the materials marketplace. Notice some track commodity indices, others track the stocks of companies involved in extracting or manufacturing basic materials. While the charts of these various ETFs are somewhat similar, the **stock-based ETFs are less volatile than ETFs that track an index.**
- **Market Leaders:** There are market leaders for most categories of basic materials and commodities and they are too numerous to discuss here. As with oil, some of the companies trade ahead of the commodity by six to nine months; others do not. Simply check their charts against the ETFs or indices for basic materials to see if they are truly ahead of the market

and therefore a good choice for a short position against a commodity market you think will come down.

Precious Metals

All that's gold does not glitter—a cliché that works. There are several ways to short precious metals, all now familiar to you, but in this segment market leaders are almost as volatile as ETFs tracking these commodities—gold, silver, platinum, and palladium.

- **Gold:** Gold trades closely alongside currencies—specifically the U.S. greenback—and in times of crisis. Fundamental demand is increasing due to increasing incomes in developing nations such as China and India. As with market segments, you can short gold by buying a put on an ETF, buying a short ETF, or buying puts on a market leader.
  - **Long ETFs:** There are two ETFs to investigate as a way to short gold. The first is the SPDR Gold Shares (GLD), which tracks the price of gold bullion. The second is the Market Vectors Gold Miners ETF (GDX), which tracks gold-mining companies. Both ETFs are liquid and have liquid puts. The gold bullion ETF (GLD) is more volatile and tracks closely to prices; the GDX is a bit ahead of bullion prices when it turns down. The chart in Figure 12.2 tells me the gold prices will be coming down.
  - **Double-Short ETFs:** The only short ETF with the kind of liquidity I like to see is the DB Gold Double Short ETF (DZZ). It tracks bullion prices closely—times two—and is a relatively new addition to the market that has already drawn a strong following after less than a year.
  - **Market Leaders:** The market leader in gold, with liquidity and market cap to go along with this position, is Barrick Gold (ABX). It tracks the GDX more closely than gold bullion prices but has a similar chart, as seen in Figure 12.2.
    With all three choices in front of you, it is clear the GDX declines more quickly when gold tumbles.
- **Silver:** Silver typically trades along with gold—the chart is almost a perfect duplicate. If for some reason you want to short silver, rather than gold, silver ETFs do not have liquid puts as I write this. There are two silver mining companies

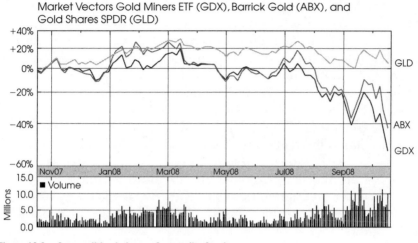

Market Vectors Gold Miners ETF (GDX), Barrick Gold (ABX), and Gold Shares SPDR (GLD)

Figure 12.2   Commodities Index vs. Commodity Stocks

Source: CSI Data

you can short: Pan American Silver (PAAS) and Silver Wheaton (SLW). They have fallen harder and deeper than the silver bullion ETF, the iShares Silver Trust (SLV).

- **Platinum:** The same is true for platinum and palladium—these metals trade as cousins. This metal is best shorted by individuals through the buying of puts on major mining companies, North American Palladium (PAL) and Stillwater Mining (SWC). Remember, platinum, a necessary ingredient in catalytic converters, also trades alongside expectations of automobile sales.

I have chosen this smallish list of ETFs and equities as a starting point if you have interest in shorting commodities. And I strongly believe and advise you that trading commodity and futures contracts is the realm of professional traders, not individual investors.

Agricultural Products

This is where it all started—commodities trading, I mean. Corn, wheat, other grains, sugar, tobacco, cotton, orange juice, the list goes on. I interviewed to be a research associate and trader at a New

York brokerage house in the late 1970s. My contact answered his phone "orange juice." The excitement I felt while walking around the brokerage's own trading floor I can still feel today. And during that interview I learned a lesson I confirmed just months ago: Individuals who trade commodities and do not do it as a full-time activity are, due to the speed of the markets and the use of leverage, likely to lose 100 percent of their money.

The treatment of the frenetic and dangerous nature of the trading of commodity contracts in the movie *Trading Places* is not too far off the mark—and the reason I urge anyone looking to make a buck by shorting these commodities to do it the simple way—with puts on ETFs and agricultural stocks even though the choices are limited. There are at this time two ETFs with sufficient liquidity in their puts.

1. **Market Vectors Agribusiness ETF (MOO):** This ETF mirrors something called the DAXglobal Agribusiness index, which in turn is based on the equities of companies that have at least 50 percent of their business in agriculture.
2. **PowerShares DB Agriculture (DBA):** The DBA tracks the longest named index I have ever come across—the Deutsche Bank Liquid Commodity Index-Optimum Yield Agriculture Excess Return. This index is based on futures contracts for commodities.

In addition, there are a great many companies near or wholly dependent on agricultural prosperity, which in turn is driven by agricultural commodity prices. Some have become surrogates for speculators, including **John Deere, Potash,** and **Monsanto.** All of these companies and the two ETFs share a common slope on their chart—with company stocks declining a bit ahead of the DBA when commodity prices turn down, showing that equity prices forecast downturns in commodity prices.

Sample Trades

Just to prove I am modest, self-effacing, and less than infallible, let's look at some of my worst recommendations ever, and let their failure be a warning to all. These two examples highlight the pitfalls of shorting hard assets.

A Commodities Trade

I and most everyone else knew steam was building up inside core commodities—basic materials, precious metals, and agriculture—markets early in 2008. My subscribers were itching to get in and sent me constant e-mails and questions. I was itching to make a trade, make a recommendation—a bad sign to begin with—and this desire alone should have given me a heads up to forget about it.

- **Mistake Number 1:** The fundamentals said it was a bubble; money flows and the charts said the bubble was not near an end. I decided to find a way to get in ahead of the blow up, against my own rule of never being the first one in.
- **Mistake Number 2:** Problems in other markets—specifically bond markets and the yen carry trade (more on that in another book) led to a short-term downturn in commodity prices as hedge funds liquidated positions to meet margin calls. I took this for a top.
- **Mistake Number 3:** Rather than pick one position where I had done overwhelming homework—which really was required since commodities were a new playing field—I recommended several positions reflecting all commodities. I recommended shorting agricultural products with an ETF and a stock, precious metals with a stock, and core commodities with an ETF. I diffused my focus and in retrospect it was because I was new to the segment.
- **Mistake Number 4:** On careful examination all three mistakes were due to my being new to the segment, and treating it like any other segment. Hard assets and commodity markets are not like equity or bond markets. I knew that and forgot about it at the same time.
- **Mistake Number 5:** I knew the bubble had to blow so I held onto the positions way too long. They all got creamed. The bubble popped later.

Bottom line: I was early, and because I had already been burned, I missed the downturn in commodities that occurred just two months later because I was gun-shy.

The Lessons: Short commodities if you know a lot about these markets. I am assuming you are not a technical or momentum trader. If you think you have learned a lot, put on a quarter or half a position to get your feet wet. In the short run, commodity markets are all about money flows and momentum—not core fundamentals. So this is all about market timing. Good luck to you.

That said, expert traders can play the volatility in these markets with things such as credit and calendar spreads, similar to the way professional traders play market indices. If that is of interest to you, there are a zillion books and online seminars that will help you learn how to lose money doing this kind of trading.

Does this mean you never short commodities?

No. Let me give you an example of where a commodity stock is tied to fundamentals. Platinum is a precious metal used in a few select products but is mostly tied to the sale of jewelry and cars in the developed world. Say what? There is platinum in every catalytic converter. If car demand and jewelry demand fall off the price should fall short term—depending on how much capacity is available in the industry. So a trade on platinum is a great collateral trade to a recession when you get your timing right and are ahead of the news in the auto sector.

Real Estate Overview

Regardless of when you read this you may want to ask "isn't shorting real estate sort of like closing the barn door after the Big Mac has been served?" My answer is: "It is always time to short a bad company in a weakening market segment." And, historically, independent of subprime mortgage troubles and real estate bubbles, there are always poor real estate investments—and short opportunities—available to individual investors when a market segment has more than 200 publicly held companies, most of them Real Estate Investment Trusts (REITs). REITs are companies that promise to pay out a certain percentage of their monthly or quarterly dividends to shareholders in return for special tax status. These profits are not taxed at the corporate level; only the shareholders are paying taxes.

There are also many collateral plays to real estate, from building suppliers and maintenance companies to mortgage lenders. I am ignoring these in this sector and focusing strictly on those companies developing, owning, and managing real estate assets.

What do I mean by real estate? There are several subsegments in this sector:

- Retail—for example, shopping malls
- Apartment buildings
- Office buildings
- Industrial properties
- Specialty commercial holdings—for example, medical offices
- Property development

Yeah, this is more complicated than you first thought. Do not be put off—the holdings of most REITs, the dominant form of equity, are transparent and you can quickly get a sense of where and what kind of properties REITs own and manage.

Real estate is also an excellent collateral play on other short positions—if growth in health care is slowing down, medical REITs may see some reduced rentals and cash flow. If consumer spending slows, shopping mall REITs may see some abandoned stores and reduced rental income. When shorting a market segment you should also check to see if there is a real estate play Wall Street has yet to discover related to that segment.

REITs are also a short-side play on rising interest rates. Most investors buy REITs because of their dividends. As the interest rates on Treasury bonds rise, REITs get hit two ways. First, their costs increase as they typically borrow money to buy and develop real estate. Second, as T-bill rates rise the spread between risk-free T-bills and the equity narrows, reducing the value of the stock.

Pick a Target—Fundamentals in Real Estate

Prospecting for shorts in real estate markets is a two-pronged exercise—examining macro factors such as interest rates and micro factors such as the regional markets served by a REIT.

Macro Factors
The macro factors at work that affect REITs come right out of an economics textbook.

- Interest rates: The lower the interest rate, the easier it is to build new buildings and the more attractive the dividend yield becomes.
- Economic growth: Slow economic growth almost always hits real estate development—the growth component of REITs— and reduces profitability.

- Demographics: Population growth, both national and regional, is the long-term driver of apartment building and retail REITs.

Micro Factors
REIT investing—and shorting—is much more bottom up than many other segments. Even during boom times would you buy a REIT with most of its assets in Detroit? Or in the 1990s who would not want to buy a medical REIT in Florida? Some factors to keep in mind:

- How pure a play is the REIT on its target sector? For example, Entertainment Properties Trust (EPR), which owns movie theaters, was a great play after 9/11. People cocoon after national trauma and in slow economic times and movie-going stays strong. When I checked them out, they were close to 100 percent invested in owning movie theaters. If they had been more diversified I might have shorted them as other forms of consumer discretionary spending pulled back in 2002 and 2003.
- How is the regional economy doing? Many REITs have heavy exposure to local economies. For example, Vornado (VNO) is heavily exposed to the office market in New York City and if you think things are going bad in and around New York, this is a good place to start your search for a specific short opportunity.
- What is their cost of capital? *All REITs are not created equal and you need to dig.* For example, some REITs pay far more interest on the money they borrow to finance new properties and expansion than others. Remember, a good component of the price of these stocks is the value of their dividend and if interest payments climb, free cash flow and dividend payments come down. This data is easy to find in financial documents and you are looking for:
  - How much debt has floating interest rates—rates can go up as well as down.
  - How much debt has a near-term (two years) termination date and needs to be replaced.
  - How much debt is fixed and long-term.

Pick a Target—Technical Indicators

In addition to all the indicators you would use as if REITs were just like any other stock, you need to look at dividends and money flows.

- **Dividends:** The value and share price of REITs is highly dependent on dividend payouts. Unlike other stocks where high-dividend yields are a sure sign of trouble, dividends confuse the issue. Remember, REITs must pay out a fixed amount of profits so if the share price falls and profits remain the same, the dividend yield is gong to increase.

  That said, **in the case of REITs, super-high dividends are a sign for you to start looking at a REIT, not confirmation the REIT is a good target**. When looking at a potential short, check to see if their dividend payments are rising or falling on a percentage yield basis. You can do this by looking at dividend payouts and divide them into share prices either monthly or quarterly. It will not take many months to establish a trend line. Commonsense math will do the rest.

  The problem for short-side investors is that dividend yields can effectively blunt the decline in a stock price for some REITs, and not for others. So be careful and unlike other stocks, high-dividend yields may be a sign that a bottom has been put in on the stock.

- **Money Flows:** There are times when high-dividend stocks come into favor and there are times they will all sell off—money is flowing in and out not due to the performance of a sector or company but due to investor caution. When markets are troubled, when geopolitical events roil markets, and when interest rates are low, dividend stocks have typically done well as a group—dry bulk shippers, Canadian gas trusts, REITs, Pfizer. Check the movement of money—look at average daily volumes or the flows into high-dividend mutual funds, or both—and do not short when there are heavy money flows into the sector.

How to Short

There are several REITs liquid enough (including their puts) for you to intelligently short this sector by shorting REITs or going back to our old reliable, ETFs.

REITs: A REIT, Real Estate Investment Trust, is an equity with special tax treatment—it avoids double taxation of profits and dividends—if it passes 90 percent of profits through to investors in the form of dividends. This sector, more than any other, provides tremendous and transparent data to the intrepid individual investor. REITs list their properties and because they pay 90 percent of their profits in dividends their financial performance is equally clear. An investor can easily determine the exposure of a REIT to a region or type of property and measure occupancy rates based on readily available data.

While there are more than 200 publicly held Real Estate Investment Trusts, few have liquid puts and these are the ones I have listed below. That said, if you are looking for a relatively manageable position of less than 50 contracts, many of the smaller REITs provide sufficient liquidity but the spreads between Bid and Ask will range from annoying to obscene.

Retail REITs

- Simon Property Group Inc. (SPG)—Shopping malls
- Kimco Realty Corporation (KIM)—Strip and shopping malls
- General Growth Properties Inc. (GGP)

Apartment REITs

- Equity Residential (EQR)
- Avalonbay Communities Inc. (AVB)
- Apartment Investment & Management Co. (AIV)

Office REITs

- Boston Properties Inc. (BXP)

Industrial REITs:

- Public Storage (PSA) (Self Storage Facilities)
- ProLogis (PLD) (Warehousing/Distribution)

Specialty REITs

- HCP, Inc. (HCP)—Medical buildings
- **Real Estate Development Companies:** These companies own and develop land while not necessarily constructing buildings. These are regional in nature and the only one with liquid puts is the St. Joe Company (JOE).
- **Long ETFs:** There is one long ETF liquid enough to short with reasonable spreads and enough outstanding contracts to move in and out of a position with relative ease—the iShares Dow Jones U.S. Real Estate (IYR).
- **Short ETFs:** There is one short ETF—it is a double-short ETF—the UltraShort Real Estate ProShares (SRS).

A Sample Trade

REITs and the ETFs based on REITs are valued, in part, based on cash flow and dividends, and sometimes they are trades that you will make due to a negative view of a market segment. Let's look at traditional consumer retail. You could short any number of companies, but want to play the segment. So you can short an ETF such as the XLY or short a REIT that owns a lot of shopping malls—you find this all out at the ETF center on Yahoo in less than 20 minutes. You think there are too many high-end retailers in the XLY that could hurt the position if high-end consumers continue to spend while low-end consumers do not. They spend money at strip malls and you find a REIT that owns malls catering to the low-end consumer. And, frankly, you are simply more comfortable with playing a company and a stock than an ETF, something you have never owned or bought a put on before.

That company, Kimco Realty, is a fairly liquid REIT. Here is what you see:

- A weakening consumer economy.
- A company that owns strip malls all over the place and uneven income. You do the same kind of analysis you would do for a company and a stock since, well, it is a company and a stock.
- There are enough puts outstanding—a few thousand—to take a small position—the puts are not very liquid but you go

forward anyway since none of the retail REITs are very liquid but you are very excited about this play on the short side of low-end consumers and retailing.

- The chart, the moving averages, and other technical indicators are looking good.
- You go ahead and buy puts that expire seven months out.

You are correct, to a point. The stock trades down almost in lock step with the XLY, the ETF for Consumer Discretionary Spending. The trade works well based on core fundamentals of the consumer market. A simple story, a simple position, a simple winning trade.

Lessons Learned: Stick to what you know, stick to rules, and if you think there is a collateral trade, don't assume the segments are linked on Wall Street even if they are linked in the real world.

Q&A

Q1. This chapter sounds like you are really down on shorting hard assets.

In abstract, the answer is no. They are valid targets. But my experience with shorting stocks and ETFs in these segments reveals they are unlike other market segments and companies. Traders need some expertise in commodities and a familiarity with Wall Street treatment of REITs before shorting these stocks and segments.

Q2. Can you give us any hints on when to time a bubble?

If I could with any degree of certainty I would be king of the world. In the history of my service the worst trades have always been related to bubbles—in 2007 it was Chinese solar stocks—and I was right about this and other bubbles but quite wrong with my timing. If you are willing to be a momentum or technical trader, there is a lot of money to be made, but I have little advice to give except get into your positions after the bubble has truly burst. And the problem with this approach is put premiums get ridiculous during bubbles and there is a limited reward for the risk you are taking.

Q3. Do you have a preference—shorting a company or an ETF when shorting hard assets?

Companies. You can do more forecasting on their performance and get a better gauge on Wall Street expectations.

Rules

- The dynamics of commodity ETFs and equities are different from other equities.
- Commodity ETFs attempt to mirror a commodity index or marketplace but you need to look at their components and performance against the price of the underlying commodities.
- Short commodities if you know a lot about these markets.
- Real estate is easily shorted by buying puts on REITs.
- Real estate is also an excellent collateral play on other short positions.
- REITs are also a short-side play on rising interest rates.
- REIT investing—and shorting—is much more bottoms up than many other segments.
- All REITs are not created equal and you need to dig.
- In the case of REITs, super-high dividends are a sign to start looking at a REIT, not confirmation the REIT is a good target.

CHAPTER

13

Shorting a Country

Why should you short a foreign stock market? You have probably heard a zillion pundits on CNBC and Fox Business talk about portfolio diversification outside the United States due to the growth of foreign markets. The inverse is true—some great short opportunities lie outside the United States as well.

Shorting a country? What I really mean, and what investors do, is short a nation's stock market. And this can be an outstanding profit generator given the volatility of many foreign markets. **Shorting a foreign market or country is by far the most complex trade with exposure to unpredictable exogenous events**. For developed foreign markets, you can short using index options in a manner similar to the way I discussed shorting market indices. Emerging markets are different and it is best to short these markets through the use of puts on long ETFs or short ETFs.

To get a good view of a foreign market, imagine a three-legged stool: a nation's bond market, a nation's currency, and a nation's economy. On closer scrutiny there is a fourth leg, sometimes seen in U.S. markets but much more noticeable overseas—especially in foreign markets—and this is the inflow (or outflow) of capital from foreign investors. Oh, and as you look at leg number four, you discover some markets have leg number five—explicit or de facto capital controls that are driving asset prices higher, artificially high.

Still interested? One last general rule: **technical indicators are much more important in shorting foreign markets, especially money flows**. Keep reading if you will.

Picking Targets

When you short a country there is a need to do some research and come up with a view of that nation, its economy, and its stock market. You should:

- Correlate trades with currency and bond market movements.
- Create a view of current and potential geopolitical events.
- Create your own view of that nation's economy and the direction of local interest rates.
- Determine Wall Street's view of that nation's economic growth, inflation rate, currency, and political stability.
- Focus more on technical indicators and momentum, especially money flows, beta, and the 200-day moving average for the relevant index or market.
- Estimate the potential for a deadly surprise.

Currency

Foreign markets create or destroy value for U.S. investors that can change based on movements in their currency against the U.S. dollar. As the dollar rises against a currency, the value of a foreign stock decreases if denominated in that currency. You will need to do some reading and look at some charts and see if the dollar is going one way or another against the local currency in the short term.

For example, a share of British Petroleum quoted as £20 is worth $40 when the pound equals $2.00. If the pound falls to $1.50 the stock is worth $30. One of the reasons foreign investors poured into the Chinese market with such intensity was the stable relationship of the Chinese currency to the dollar—they knew their positions would not be hit, short term, by the dollar falling against the renminbi. Or is the yuan? See what I mean about complexity—China has two currencies, one for insiders, one for outsiders.

The current and future value of a nation's currency is reflected and forecast by trends in market for that nation's bonds unless they are denominated in U.S. dollars.

Geopolitical Events

While these are impossible to predict—who could have predicted Russia would invade Georgia?—you can create a view to shape your position. Ask the following questions:

- Will the target nation's stock market move based on a significant geopolitical event? There is no formula. It depends on the event and the market. That said, the less developed or smaller the market, the more likely money will flow out. Also, an event can really be a series of events such as the machinations of Hugo Chavez to become the 21st-century's version of Benito Mussolini by nationalizing companies and making his society more and more authoritarian. This has led to a sell-off in Venezuelan shares and declines in ETFs with these shares among their components.
- What possible events or changes in political direction could hit the country? This is all about reading, visiting the country, having family and friends in country—all are great sources of insight.
- What is the trend line for stability for the country? Venezuela is a good example. It has steadily deteriorated and my dog could draw a trend line showing things are probably going to get worse.

Economic Growth

There is probably too much information from too many sources about other countries. Check out a few websites such as the International Monetary Fund (IMF) and the Financial Times and just roam around until you get comfortable with data sources you find credible. And remember Chinese government data is about as reliable as what you last read in a fortune cookie.

Wall Street's View

Go to Google, find some analysts knowledgeable with the country in question, and see what they are saying. Shy away from comments by fund managers actively invested in the country—they are always spinning out good news. Listen to comments by fund managers who do asset allocation and are agnostic about one specific country or region.

Capital Controls

Wall Street analysts smile their way to you on TV—I do it, too, so I am truly making fun of everyone—but they typically avoid discussions of factors that artificially inflate asset prices in another country. The most common contributor is a constricted flow of capital out of the country—capital controls or prohibitions against citizens investing in foreign markets or some combination of the two. The best thing about **capital controls is how they create stock market bubbles that are, when properly timed, great opportunities for short side investors**.

This happened in Japan in the late 1980s and is happening in China right now. Simply put, these nations—and others—are net exporters and foreign currency enters their country, which becomes savings. Air is coming into the balloon. The nations discourage or prohibit this money from being sent overseas, so these savings—another name for investment capital—stays domestic and has to be put to work. It is invested, over and over, in domestic assets, including bonds, which makes borrowing cheap, creating more capital to be invested in these markets or in cheap industrial capacity, creating more exports, and so on. The balloon keeps getting bigger until an exogenous event, a trade war, or something else pops the balloon. The Nikkei, the primary Japanese stock market index, was around 39,000 when I lived in Tokyo in 1989; it was below 10,000 not too long ago. What a short!

Technical Indicators

Developed markets in Europe and Japan generate familiar technical indicators and emerging markets such as China, India, and Russia have charts that have much sharper ups and downs. Developed markets move on fundamentals and the occasional spurt of foreign investment. Markets in developing nations move, short term, on money flows from foreign investors with fundamentals coming in a distant second. **Capital inflows distort and often drive the valuation and performance of foreign markets, especially emerging markets**.

How much foreign money is in the market or flowing in and out of the market? Quick Google searches will tell you how much foreign money—typically U.S. and European money—is in the stock market of a country. Even in places where foreigners have ownership restrictions, such as India, foreign money is put to work with local partners and can leave at a moment's notice.

Deadly Surprises

In early 2008 if you had followed charts and shorted China through ETFs holding Hong Kong stocks, your logic might have won an award but you would have been creamed. Why? Around that time the Chinese government put new restrictions on mainland stock markets and money flowed directly into the Hong Kong market. Your position would have blown up—even though mainland markets were cratering. A true deadly surprise. There is no rule of thumb here, just do your homework and if you see there is too much you cannot see, you may want to avoid shorting that country.

How to Short

There are various ways in which to short a country. They vary based on whether the market in that country is developed or is considered an emerging market.

Developed Markets

Shorting a developed market—in the United Kingdom, in France, in Germany—is similar to shorting the S&P 500 using puts on the major indices in three countries or ETFs that track these indices.

Shorting developed countries involves understanding anywhere from three to five aspects of a country: its markets, economy, currency, capital inflows, and capital controls.

The major markets in Europe have indices that can be traded with index options: the British (FTSE 100), French (CAC 40), and German (DAX 30). They are not nearly as liquid as index options on the Dow, S&P, or NASDAQ, but they can still be traded by individuals.

There are also ETFs for all developed nations, for just Europe, for just Japan, as well as on specific market indices. Some of these, such as the iShares MSCI EAFE Index (EFA), an ETF for the 21 indices for developed nations, have liquid puts but most of these ETFs do not. The list grows every day and most broker and financial sites keep up-to-date lists.

Another approach is to short ADRs of companies that are part of that nation's market index and likely to suffer when a country's economy goes south.

Be aware that most European markets follow each other in the short term, as do Asian markets, but in the long run they can and will diverge. Keep this in mind when looking at shorting more than one market.

Emerging Markets

Emerging markets are the lands of puts on long ETFs and short or inverse ETFs. Liquidity is not an issue for short ETFs as you are not buying options; liquidity of puts is an issue for all but a couple of long ETFs. The number of ETFs is increasing daily but the ETFs that stand out now are the UltraShort MSCI Emerging Markets ProShares (EEV), a double-short ETF that covers all emerging markets. There is also a double-short ETF for China—the UltraShort FTSE/Xinhua China 25 Proshare (FXP). Remember, **ETFs do not always mirror market indices on a day-to-day basis—you need to track their histories and see how they diverge**.

There are also ADRs available for companies in emerging markets, mostly in the BRIC markets: Brazil, Russia, India, and China.

A Sample Trade

It starts in May 2008 with a dinner with a friend in the garment business who is supplied from factories in China. Your friend Laura comes back from China and says business is terrible—her supplier is complaining about rising labor costs, a rising currency, new government regulations, increased shipping charges, and cancelled orders, with no upside. You spring for a nice bottle of wine and it is time to do some prospecting and analysis.

This is how many great trades start—the Peter Lynch/personal knowledge approach. This is even more true for people looking at foreign markets. For example, I was in Paris, London, and Edinburgh at the end of July 2008. I always ask a lot of questions when I travel around the question "how is business." The answer was "awful, awful, and pretty good," which made sense as Edinburgh is a much cheaper destination than Paris or London. Less than two weeks after I got back the EU announced the single sharpest year-over-year drop in consumer spending since they began collecting data. Personal observations matter. Your conclusion: the Chinese economy is slowing faster than Wall Street thinks it is slowing.

Time to shape a trade.

Step 1: In this case, you start with your friend's telling you business in China is weakening. And you begin to read—everything, from *USA Today* to specialized websites about the economy in China, with the best coverage coming from the *Wall Street Journal Asia* (you buy a trial subscription) and the *Economist.* And the observations of their reporters support Laura's comments. You find support for your previous conclusion—the Chinese economy is slowing faster than Wall Street thinks it is slowing.

Step 2: You have read Chinese markets and stocks cannot directly be shorted—so how will you short the market? You discover several long ETFs and a short- and a double-short ETF. And start digging.

Step 3: The digging reveals these ETFs mirror either Hong Kong stocks, ADRs of Chinese companies listed in the United States, or the performance of multinational companies with heavy exposure to China. Your initial enthusiasm turns to dismay—you actually cannot short domestic Chinese markets that have already cratered and seem to be sliding every day. A check of the chart for the double-short RTF—the FXP or UltraShort FTSE/Xinhua China 25 Proshare—shows it has actually fallen and just climbed back and has not tracked the mainland Chinese stock markets at all. **You turn to ADRs.**

Step 4: This is a wrong turn: You discover more than 75 ADRs and there is too little research available to give you a feel for what is great trade—you have read my book and are looking for a great trade!—and you kick back and turn again to your macro scenario—the Chinese economy is slowing more than people think. And from that, you make a discovery: dry-bulk shippers.

Step 5: The real step four: China imports huge amounts of raw materials and this has driven a dramatic rise in shipping rates—and in the value of a category of company called a dry-bulk shipper. Bingo! You like this segment for the following reasons:

- They are a pure play not just on a Chinese economic slow-down but any worldwide slowdown—and you believe one is coming.
- The two companies you look at hard—Diana Shipping (DSX) and Eagle Bulk Shipping (EGLE)—have transparent financials and pay huge dividends that, when cut due to slowing economic conditions and falling rates and utilization, immediately hit the stock. You discover these dividend payouts are not a bribe—they are common to all bulk carrier companies due to their former ownership structure as partnerships.
- Shipping rates can be tracked daily and there are several websites that summarize rates weekly and monthly as well as capacity and long versus spot rates, creating an environment where there are few gigantic financial surprises.
- Technical indicators are all flashing green—the stocks are breaking down as shown in Figure 13.1.
- You still feel a bit unfamiliar with the segment so you decide to take half a position in puts on each company. The put/call ratio is very bullish—far more calls than puts—and

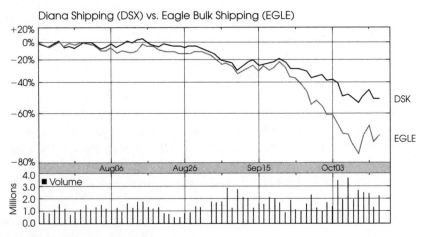

Figure 13.1   Stocks Breaking Down

Source: CSI Data

you discover this too is common with high-dividend paying stocks and the put/call ratios for these stocks are not unusual.

- You buy puts seven months out—plenty of time for the puts to survive any technical bounces—and they get hit a few weeks after you put the trade on. Eventually you get your double, roll the position, and get another double before you close the position.

Conclusion

Unless you are a momentum or technical trader you need a deep understanding of the country you intend to short, or its markets, or both. I found as a relatively new trader my experience was similar to what happened to me when I established short positions in real estate and commodities—I treated the trade too much as a traditional equity or ETF for a market segment. Have I exaggerated the difficulty here and in the chapter on shorting hard assets? No—commodities and countries are not companies and stocks. Start with that premise, and realize you need to accumulate different kinds of knowledge before you can make some serious profits.

Q&A

Q1. Are there any websites or other information sources you like for doing research about specific nations?

I would begin with the free component of the *Financial Times*—maybe even spring for a subscription. Then head to Yahoo and Google and start trolling around. A good search term in addition to the country name is "market intelligence"; you should also try "geopolitical risk" and "economic forecasts."

Q2. Are European market indices as easy to short as American indices?

Yes, depending on what broker you use. Puts on the major indices are liquid and easily tradeable.

Q3. Do ETFs truly mirror markets or do they occasionally diverge?

Yes and no—you need to trace the performance of an ETF against the market index it is supposed to track.

Rules

- Shorting a foreign market or country is by far the most complex trade with exposure to unpredictable exogenous events.
- Technical indicators are much more important in shorting foreign markets, especially money flows.
- Foreign markets create or destroy value for U.S. investors that can change based on movements in their currency against the U.S. dollar.
- Shorting a developed market—in the U.K., in France, in Germany—is similar to shorting the S&P 500 using puts on the major indices in three countries or ETFs that track these indices.
- Shorting countries involves understanding from three to five aspects of a country: its markets, economy, currency, capital inflows, and capital controls.
- Capital inflows distort and often drive the valuation and performance of foreign markets, especially emerging markets.
- ETFs do not always mirror market indices on a day-to-day basis—you need to track their histories and see how they diverge.

CHAPTER

14

Shorting in a Bull Market

Too many e-mails and questions from traders attending my seminars revolve around the same question—"the market is running, should I short this stock or segment?" The answer is always the same: the best method to short is based on fundamentals, not momentum. But it can be much more difficult when a rapidly rising tide lifts all boats. You can make money when the bull takes charge—you just need to stay focused, disciplined, and be more selective.

This is a brief chapter because all the tactics you require to short a stock or market segment in a bull rally have been discussed somewhere else. You know what to do, but when buying puts during a bull market rally, you need to be even more selective and pay more attention to day-to-day movements in these puts than under other market conditions.

What are the ways to short in a bull market? I prefer two basic methods, and each has tremendous profit potential depending on your risk tolerance. These are the fundamental shorts—that would-be Pfizer with terrible financial prospects in any market or the purchase of puts on short ETFs. These ETFs go down, fast, when the segment or index they inversely mirror goes up.

First, some cautionary words. When Alan Greenspan liquefied the world with floods of cash near the end of 1999—in case the banking system was hit by some Y2K conversion problem—the NASDAQ doubled from August 1999 to February 2000 and to get in front of this freight train one would have had to be insane. Arguably this is a once-in-a-generation event, but **no method**

for shorting has a reasonable chance of succeeding in the face of this kind of a raging bull market. The typical bull rally pushes stocks much more slowly than this kind of run—and in a typically bull rally you can short a lousy company and stock with some confidence.

What is a bull rally? A 20 percent move—my definition—in six months or less. If you are in the middle of one, the market probably has not hit that 20 percent target, but if the chart shows it is clearly headed in that direction, assume you are in the middle of one.

What do you do when you see a great opportunity—an individual stock—in a bull rally?

- Do the fundamental analysis of the opportunity discussed in the previous chapters.
- Compare the movement of the stock versus the movement of the segment the company is in, such as Pfizer in the pharmaceutical industry. If the entire segment is flat, lagging, or trading against the general market, consider this a positive sign for the position.
- Check technical indicators—twice. Take a look at the 50- and 200-day moving averages as if you were in a stable market and as suggested in Chapter 5 on technical indicators. Then track these against the 50- and 200-day moving averages of the markets in general. You should not begin creating a position unless the stock is at or has broken these averages and the chart shows the ability to trade against the markets. By this I mean the direction of the market is clearly up and the chart of the stock is lagging, flat, or is going down compared to the market. Also look for declining volume compared to volume movements in the general markets.
- Check the put/call ratio for the stock and for the indices. The put/call ratio should be more biased—a little bit—toward puts than for the general market.

Let's look at an example—this is not a recommendation, just an example—IHOP, my "favorite breakfast without the kids while they are playing winter lacrosse" eatery. A good outfit—in a crowded market. Let's say the market is rising rapidly, consumer spending data shows the consumer is feeling good, and restaurant stocks are rising, but you don't see how IHOP is going to absorb

Applebee's (it bought Applebee's in 2007) and make profits to support its stock price.

- Your fundamental look at the company tells you the market is too crowded and profit margins are falling.
- The stock is trading up, but not nearly as fast as the market. It is up 4 percent in the past 90 days while the market is up 16 percent.
- You check other restaurant chains—Ruby Tuesday, a direct competitor, Cheesecake Factory, a cut above, and McDonald's, a cut below—and they are all up at least 9 percent.
- Average daily volume is flat—while volume in other restaurants and the general markets is increasing. The put/call ratio is also more negative than for the general market.
- All technical indicators are flashing green—make the trade.

Some other thoughts: **Put premiums, across the board, are typically lower during a bull rally**. This is a rough rule of thumb—prices should be different stock by stock—but my experience shows this to be true a good part of the time. **Stocks fall fast near the end of a bull rally as they are stretched and traders are quick to take profits in anticipation of a stock decline**. And while I caution the need for more selectivity and greater attention to technical indicators, **the potential reward is really great as you are truly trading against the market**.

Another way to make money—a higher-risk way—is to buy puts on a short ETF or, better yet, a double-short ETF. You already know all about this if you have read the section on shorting a market segment. There are many ETFs that are designed to short various market segments, and you can buy puts on these that are liquid and trade like regular puts. What do you do?

- Use the same approach to analyze fundamentals you have used for shorting a market segment in a regular market.
- Look for the same clear technical signs I described earlier, and **when buying puts on a short ETF, focus on the moving averages and the put/call ratio on the ETF in question. With an ETF of a market segment, a technical movement moving faster than the general markets is an even stronger sign of potential profit than the movement of an individual stock.**

- **Managing a put position on a short or double-short ETF requires constant attention**. When buying puts on a short ETF, you can literally get a 100 percent gain in day or two. Or lose 80 percent of the value. **When buying puts on a short ETF, I urge you to consider using trailing sell stops on profitable positions** and to stick to price targets—take profits quickly and simply reopen or roll the position as you see fit and if the fundamentals continue in your favor.

Conclusion

I am a natural contrarian and these, personally, are my kind of trades: to go against the grain, to go against the conventional wisdom, not just for the psychic satisfaction when I am proven right but also because shorting a stock in a bull market rally—or a market segment—can create some of the largest and fastest profits among all your short positions. Doing this is also inherently riskier than when markets are stable or declining. With technical indicators being more important under these conditions the key here is discipline—a stock can trade irrationally, away from fundamentals, in a bull market rally—and paying close attention to your positions.

Q&A

Q1. How do I "find the nerve" to short in a bull market rally?

You don't. Do not push yourself or go outside of your comfort zone to trade against a bull rally, which is a formula for disaster. If a trade under bull-rally conditions keeps you up at night or makes you nervous—more nervous than any other trade—stay away.

Q2. Why do you characterize a bull rally by the market going up 20 percent?

You gotta start somewhere, and since I am a simple guy, I opted for the inverse of the definition of a bear market decline, which is a market that declines 20 percent. More importantly, many others see the same 20 percent as a potential end of a rally and many technical traders move in and out of the indices and stocks based on this assumption.

Q3. Would you consider using sell stops on puts on short ETFs?

I would use trailing sell stops on profitable positions, but if you put in a sell stop when you create a position, you greatly increase the likelihood of taking a loss because of the volatility of these puts and being stopped out of a position.

Rules

- No method for shorting has a reasonable chance of succeeding in the face of a raging bull market such as year-end 1999.
- Put premiums, across the board, are typically lower during a bull rally.
- Stocks fall fast near the end of a bull rally as they are stretched and traders are quick to take profits in anticipation of a stock decline.
- When buying puts on a short ETF, focus on the moving averages and the put/call ratio for the ETF in question.
- Managing a put position on a short or double-short ETF requires constant attention.
- When buying puts on a short ETF, I urge you to consider using trailing sell stops on profitable positions.
- Do not push yourself or go outside of your comfort zone to trade against a bull rally, which is a formula for disaster.

CHAPTER

Advanced Trading Techniques

As I have said more than once, there have been many books and dissertations written on advanced trading techniques of options. This is a brief look at several simple and effective ways to sell short using options. My review is just that, a review, not an instruction manual, and I have focused on techniques that complement all that has been discussed in prior chapters.

A quick thought: **If you are uncomfortable with advanced trading techniques but they intrigue you, try dry trading for a while—set up a dummy account somewhere and trade without real money for a while to see how it goes.**

Selling Calls

You would be surprised by how many long investors refuse to generate cash by selling calls. This is a simple way to play the short side of a stock you are really bullish on in the long term. Suppose you own a stock you fear will take a hit but do not want to sell for any number of reasons. You sell calls—the right to buy the stock at a fixed price on or before a future date. For example, let's say I own Gilead Sciences and see $55 as a short-term ceiling. I sell the $60 call with an expiration date about nine weeks from now and generate $2.30, a rich premium.

- If the stock does not rise to $60 I let the call expire and I do it all over again—perhaps the next time it will be the $65 call because the stock has begun to rise again.
- If the stock falls and the value of the call falls sharply—let's say a buck—I will buy the call back and cover my position, closing it. My profit is the $1.30.
- The stock moves and I get called out—someone exercises the option and buys the stock for $60. My net price is $62.30—the value of the stock plus what I received for the call—a 13 percent gain in nine weeks.

Hedging

To hedge is more than a verb describing the day-to-day activities of politicians—it is a method for insulating a position or portfolio from a short-term downturn in price.

The first step when hedging is to sell calls and generate cash.

Let's go back to Gilead. You have only owned it three months, it has gone from $47 to $57, and you want to hold on for another six months to get long-term capital gains treatment. The stock is at $57 and you sell $55 calls for six months out for $6.10. You take that $6.10 and buy a $55 put on your position for $4.

You have locked in the value of the stock at $55 for six months. The only financial risk is if the stock blows up, and you end up with a valuable put, you will pay short-term capital gains taxes on the profits from the put.

There are numerous variations of this strategy. For instance:

- You are long—you are always long—and you sense the market is going down for a few months. The kids are going off to college and you do not want your portfolio's value to fall too sharply but you mostly own income stocks whose dividends are going to pay, in part, for college.
- You take some cash and buy puts on the S&P 500, SPX puts. Your portfolio is worth $250,000.
- Let's say the S&P 500 is trading at 1300 with the SPX at 130. You are afraid of a 15 percent correction—I don't know why; this is long-term money and you own stable companies with dividend-paying stocks, but it is your life—anyway, you go out

and consider buying SPX puts at the 110 strike price that, if they hit the strike price, will be worth $50,000.

- This is going to cost you a bundle if you do it four times a year—about 1.5 percent of the value of your portfolio every three months, so if you do this a year you will wipe out your dividend gains. You decide to buy puts that will hedge 50 percent of your portfolio.

I cringe when I read this but there is a method to this madness—that is, to inform you hedging is not as simple as it seems.

The proper move for this investor was to hedge each dividend-paying stock, in effect turning them into a bond. Sell a call, buy a put, lock in a price and the dividend.

There are a zillion ways to hedge a portfolio. My preferred method is to have core holdings that typically command solid or high premiums for their calls, sell calls on half the portfolio and use this to buy S&P puts for between half and all of your portfolio. This takes some work but it is possible. The weakness in this method is that stocks with high-call premiums typically are more volatile than the general market and logically could or should fall harder than the averages, which means the puts you buy may not rise in value equal to what you lose on your stocks.

Where am I going with this? If you want to hedge, and you do not have the time available to a professional investor, do one of two things:

1. **Take the simple way out:** Hedge individual stocks.
2. **Make a trade:** Buy puts on the S&P as if they were a stand-alone trade using the methods discussed throughout this book. Do not try to calibrate the position size—how much the puts will pay if you hit your target price—to how much your portfolio will lose if the market falls as expected. Manage this as an independent trade. You will manage it better if you do not constantly refer back to the value of your long portfolio.

Bear Call Spreads

This is a technique used by many day- and short-term traders to hit lots and lots of singles, with occasional home runs, while playing a downward swing in the market. This technique requires trading discipline and the use of automatic sell prices and stop losses. This brief explanation is just that, an explanation, not a tutorial, and for more information check out the Chicago Board Options Exchange website for online courses and tutorials, plus sites sponsored by brokers and trading services.

The easiest way to explain this kind of trade is to walk you through one.

Step 1: You decide Gilead is going down in the next few months because you believe sales of its HIV drugs will slow (you are nuts, but this is just an example).

Step 2: You first play defense and allocate 2 percent of your portfolio and tell yourself to set up a trade to play great defense.

Step 3: You establish your time horizon as close in—four weeks—as this is when you go on vacation. Another bad input into the trade but let's roll with it.

Step 4: You look at several factors:
- The current value of the stock: $50.
- Potential exogenous factors—it is early July, the international AIDs conference is upcoming, and Gilead is going to get bashed again as activists believe its drugs cost too much.
- You look at premiums on various calls and see the market agrees with your assessment. They are typically high for Gilead and this month is no exception.

You then go for it, creating a Bear Call Spread around the $50 price point. These are also called credit spreads as you receive a credit or net cash inflow when you first execute the trade.

- Gilead is selling for $50 a share. One month out, the call option for the strike price of $52.50 is selling for $1 and the call option for $47.50 is selling for $3.50.
- You buy the $52.50 call (costing you $100) and you sell the $47.50 calls and collect $350. Your net at the moment is $250.
- The stock closes at $50 and the call is not exercised. You are up $250.
- You have a loss if the stock closes at or above $105. You would then sell shares at $47.50, buy the shares at $52.50, and deliver them. Your loss would be $5 a share minus what you

had put in your pocket—$2.50. So your potential loss is equal to your potential gain.

There are so many variations of this simple trade I get a headache thinking about it. I have used the S&P as the example but you can do these spreads on almost anything. You manage this kind of a position with firm stop losses and target prices.

Selling Puts on Short ETFs

ETFs that are short something—a market segment or market index—go up in value as that segment or index falls. A conservative way to play the upside with these ETFs is to sell puts. This strategy is best used when you have a longer term view of the market segment.

For example, you are convinced the banks are going to be in trouble for at least several quarters. You want to play this through the double-short ETF on banks, the SKF. But you are a most conservative person—your husband is the big shot gambler who plays nickel poker every Friday night—and the volatility in the SKF is daunting. So, convinced it is great long-term play but concerned about the week-by-week volatility, you sell puts.

- The SKF is at $150 and can move 7 percent to 10 percent in a day. You sell the $130 put for $5 with an expiration date five weeks out.
- If the ETF continues to rise or stay where it is, or even decline to $131, the put will expire worthless. You believe this will happen because the ETF rises as the financials fall in value.
- If you are wrong in the short term, and the ETF falls to $125, you have to buy the SKF at $130. At this price you are net even because you pocketed $5 when you sold the put. Anything below $125 and you start losing money—temporarily.
- Why temporarily? Because you don't mind owning the SKF as your long-term view has the financials falling for quite a while.

Most brokers require you have enough capital in your account to buy the puts if they are put to you.

Short Straddles

These are incredibly risky as they have unlimited liability similar to a traditional short position but with the added risk of leverage! How about a definition and we will leave it that? Good—here we go—a short straddle is agnostic—it does not assume the stock or market is going up or down and actually makes the most money when the stock or market goes perfectly sideways. In this approach the insane trader sells a put and call for the same date and strike price at the same time. The profit potential on this trade can be no greater than the cash generated by the sale of the put and call—the loss, as you can guess, is unlimited if the stock moves sharply in either direction.

Stay away.

The Rocket-Fueled Trade

I have described this in Chapter 14 but want to review it again. This is the purchase of a call on a double-short ETF. I know of no other trade readily available to individual investors with this kind of leverage and such a favorable risk/reward ratio. I am not saying this kind of trade is for everyone or for anything but the most speculative part of your portfolio—but it is something to consider.

- Let's say you really are an expert on China—you do business there and you see the three companies manufacturing the products for your American-based clothing company are struggling. They are caught between rising costs and competition from cheaper countries you just visited, Bangladesh and Vietnam. You turned down the tickets for Olympics as did all the other people you know doing business in China. Your hotel, where you stay four times a year, is half empty; you have no trouble getting a taxi or a table at your favorite restaurant.
- You check out the market and see it is way down. The double-short ETF is the only option and it is focused on Hong Kong stocks. You make some calls, Hong Kong companies are in trouble as well and you decide to go short. But you want to do it big time.

- You find a double-short ETF, the FXP. Let's say it is selling for $100. You look at calls five months out and the $130 calls are selling for $15. Too expensive—that presumes a 22.5 percent decline in the market for you to break even at expiration. But you believe things will get very bad. You look short term instead—six weeks with expiration after the Olympics. With the ETF at $100, the $120 calls are $4.75. If the market goes down 10 percent, the call will be at breakeven.

You walk away from the trade. The risk-reward ratio is very unfavorable so you look elsewhere. Your husband, the nickel poker player, sells software and has several clients that are banks.

They are not buying; they are not hiring; they are doing nothing. You turn to the financials, and do a couple of days of reading, call the two banks you use, and decide there is no turnaround in sight. You find the SKF, the double-short ETF in the financial sector.

- The ETF is at $150.
- You look at a chart and historical prices and see the ETF can move 10 percent a day even when the market is calm.
- Calls expiring three months out are too expensive; you look at September calls. The $170 calls are selling for $3. Financials would have to fall 11.5 percent—theoretically—for this to break even.
- You check the charts again and the sector is about 6 percent off their previous lows and headed back there in a hurry. A 6 percent move in a week or two would push the ETF to $168 and, at $168, and with little time decay, the calls could explode.
- You are usually not a short-term trader but this looks good. You are chicken—as well you should be—and put up 1 percent of your trading portfolio.
- Six trading days later the ETF is at $169 and the puts are selling for $20—a 650 percent–plus gain.
- A market move of 6 percent has just produced a gain of 650 percent in six days: a true rocket-fueled trade.

What I like most is the risk/reward profile of this trade. If the market segment had moved in the other direction 6 percent, and the ETF fell to $132, the call, which still had almost three weeks before expiration, would have lost no more than 50 percent to 65 percent of its value due to volatility in the sector creating residual value in even way out of the money puts. If you use this technique, I would also use trailing stop losses after you have made a serious profit—what that level might be is up to you.

Conclusion

Keep it simple when using slightly more advanced techniques. As your skills and profits grow, you can move on, but starting too fast is a recipe for disaster. I have a money manger for part of my portfolio who does nothing but trade credit spreads on the S&P. He did 27 percent in the past 12 months, something I could not do without years of experience and time. He has made 1,100 trades in the first seven months of this year!

Simple is not the same thing as conservative. There are times to be more aggressive, and there are also times to be more conservative. The simple techniques discussed in this chapter will let you do both.

Q&A

Q1. Can I use bear call spreads on market indices?

Ubet. And using credit spreads on the SPX is much more efficient than credit spreads for stocks due to liquidity—there is a lower cost with SPX calls than with calls on equities.

Q2. The rocket-fueled trade—how large a position should I create?

I smell greed—and I should be smelling fear as well. This is a high-risk trade, despite the favorable risk/reward ratio. I would stick with whatever portfolio allocation mechanism you use and then adjust that for the higher risk. Yes, no firm answer coming from moi except play defense first.

(Continued)

Q3. Does hedging really work?

Yes, but you have to work at it. In 2003 when the market was rocking and rolling up and down—at least my positions were—I made an extra seven points of return by selling calls. I only used some of that cash to buy puts, some of it to buy more shares.

Rules

- If you are uncomfortable with advanced trading techniques but they intrigue you, try dry trading for a while. Set up a dummy account somewhere to use a pad and paper and trade without real money for a while to see how it goes.

Case Studies—Ruby Tuesday, the Bear, and the Home Builders

I have alluded to but not provided a great deal of detail on three of my better trades—trades recommended to my subscribers, not personal trades—Ruby Tuesday, Bear Stearns, and the home builders.

Ruby Tuesday

I love this trade because it is a perfect blend of using instinct, hard data, and effective position management to create a terrific profit.

Why RT?

- I stopped into a Ruby Tuesday for some forgotten reason with one of my sons—we typically eat there when on the road—and noticed (a) a paucity of diners, and (b) lots of coupons and discounted specials.
- I asked the ChangeWave Research survey group to tack some questions on restaurants onto the next Consumer Spending survey.
- I began trolling the Web for third-party data on restaurant spending in the casual dining market segment. I learned the number of stores had grown 17 percent in the past three years despite stalled income growth and an obviously much smaller growth in the dining population. Most analysts felt the segment was overcrowded with "me too" chains and menus and felt some weaker outfits would begin to struggle. The entire

segment was headed down—including RT—but the chain was thought to be well-positioned if there was shakeout.

- I sensed it had to lose big time. I saw it in person, margins had to fall due to price wars and couponing against weaker competitors who would degrade prices in the segment. Not to mention lots of empty tables. I visited a couple more RTs in my area and the crowds were underwhelming.

- Perfect. Macro forces in the economy plus too much competition plus a favorable (and misguided) set of opinions on Wall Street.

- Technical indicators said I had a clear shot at a great trade— the charts and other indicators said there was nothing to get in the way of the trade.

- Time to go short. Even though my kids love the ribs and I am partial to their pretty-good salad bar.

This trade went as follows:

On October 25, with the stock at $15.61 I quickly settled on the January 2008 $15 puts—they were reasonably priced at $1.05. Lots of leverage, a good chance for a double; they had just announced earnings two weeks before and the stock was beginning to slide. One month later, on November 27, I rolled the position—the stock was at $13.40, I closed the position at $2.10, a 100 percent gain but kept subscribers in the trade.

At $13.40, the chart was a dream, earnings were not for a few more weeks and ChangeWave data showed an ever weakening consumer and a pullback on restaurant spending. The story was still intact. I held this position through the New Year and rolled it again on January 3 when the stock was trading at $9.18 and the puts were worth $3.60—a 177 percent gain.

On that day, January 3, 2008, the market had yet to react to a potentially weak holiday season. ChangeWave Research survey data and visits to restaurants told me Santa had gotten stuck in the chimney. I saw the story was intact and recommended buying the July $7.50 put at $0.75. A few days later holiday sales data began to come in for stores and restaurants and the stock blew up. The stock cracked down to $6.01 and I closed this one-week-old position at $2.60—a 247 percent gain in a week.

The stock had fallen from $15.61 to $6.01—a drop of 61 percent. Wow. The three positions—rolled, with subs being told to pull profits out and reinvest only the original capital—produced gains of 524 percent. If my subscribers were more aggressive than I am and pressed their profits back into the trade, their return would have been $19 for the $1 they invested.

I chose to focus on this trade because it is the great example of the slam dunk:

- **Personal data:** Empty restaurants with too many coupons.
- **Great third-party data:** The industry and ChangeWave Research survey data were flawless.
- **The puts were always reasonably priced.**
- **The technical indicators were behind the trade.**

Why did I close it out? I thought there was no more room to run. The stock was stabilizing as Wall Street had now completely absorbed bad news and weakening forecasts. The company is well-managed and was not going bankrupt. There would be little the company could do to present a downside surprise to the Street going forward. (I was wrong—as I write this the stock is below $2. But the trade still made a great profit and I am happy to make mistakes leaving profits on the table as compared to making mistakes and leaving my core capital in the trash.)

Lesson Learned: If the fundamentals hold, keep pushing, press on and protect your capital as you see fit. But keep going for home runs when profits are coming your way.

Bear Stearns

My recommending puts on Bear Stearns is an example of, a) picking the perfect intersection of a weakening company and a weakening segment, and, b) having the discipline to close a trade in the middle of chaos. Bear, to-date, is my most visible success despite it not being my biggest gainer—and it almost did not happen.

Why did I pick Bear?

- I had learned enough to know the mortgage mess was hitting many banks—I had already shorted Citi—and I was looking for the firm with the most exposure.

- My dog Sumo knew Bear had heavy exposure to lousy mortgages based on headlines and the collapse of two hedge funds—managed by Bear—in the summer of 2007, the event some now see as the trigger for the entire credit crunch.
- If the numbers being kicked around Bear were correct, and the quality of the subprime loans it held on its books mirrored what was in the hedge funds, the company was toast.
- I sensed an intangible that the typical individual investor might not be able to factor in—Bear was a universally detested firm on Wall Street and I knew that if they ran into trouble none of their peers were going to cut them any slack. They were famous for having a "take no prisoners" approach to business and reinforced this in the 1990s by being one of the few banks not to heed the Fed and help with the bailout of Long Term Capital. Turns out this was even more true than I expected.
- The Fed had no history of bailing out an investment bank and did not provide liquidity to investment banks in trouble—at that time.
- The stock had only sporadic support and all the technical indicators were saying full speed ahead—and down. And, on the day I recommended the position, March 10, put volume exploded—people were anticipating something might happen that week.
- Time to go short.

Finding the right put was an uncomfortable exercise as premiums seemed to expand every minute. I finally chose the July $50 puts—trading at $5.70—as the stock traded around $60. Put premiums were exploding and this had the most reasonable risk/reward ratio; even $30 puts had stiff premiums on March 10. But this was a prelude of what was to come.

The week of March 10 saw a great deal of sentiment move against Bear and a lot of it was in the press. The puts were moving up in value but the stock was poised to go off a cliff. Chaos was setting in and spreads were widening on the puts, a good sign. On the morning of March 14 as I listened to CNBC for premarket chatter, things were not looking good, and I alerted my editor we might be getting out—chaos works two ways and I felt if Bear fell too far someone would come in and take them out. I got picked up for my regular 10 A.M. gig on Fox Business, did the makeup thing, and walked into the studio. All hell had broken loose, the stock had been in free fall at the open and was now struggling to make a comeback. With the director politely informing me I had a couple of minutes before the camera came to me I typed an alert on my Blackberry, which told my subscribers to get out at market; we had a near 300 percent gain and who knew what this chaos could produce to wipe out our gains. When the market closed I was happy. My timing seemed very good indeed.

We had a 287 percent gain—and then on Monday morning Bear was officially shot; the company was bought at $2 a share. The 287 percent gain would have been north of 840 percent if I had kept the position open.

Why did I close it out and not roll it or press it? In a word, trading chaos—well, two words, actually—the spreads between the Bid and the Ask for puts in the middle of the chaos on March 14 were impossible to manage and put buyers were getting whipsawed. No way am I going to ask my subscribers to trade in the middle of that kind of insanity. I was also concerned about an exogenous event destroying the position—actions by the Fed or an acquisition or capital infusion. Turns out I was right, but who could see the price being $2 a share (eventually raised to $10).

Lesson Learned: Be a pig but not a stupid one. In the face of chaos, take profits and a deep breath before doing anything new like rolling or pressing a position.

The Home Builders

Shorting the home builders was not the slam dunk you might think and this trade is a great example of, a)acting on third-party opinion, b)sticking with a position through a big rally in the stocks, and, c)playing a segment with a series of individual puts on stocks, not an ETF or index. The home builders have driven me nuts for many months and I like to refer back to this trade to reinforce the message of patience and "volatility is not risk."

Why the home builders? I have made lighthearted comments about using lunches with smart people as an investment tool but this is absolutely the case with how I first put home builders on my horizon in the first quarter of 2007. I, like many other people, thought I had missed their fall. I also could not turn to my constant data source—ChangeWave surveys—as we do not cover home purchases or building. My source, a broker/analyst at a major investment bank, was not a Wall Street person—she was a local broker who happened to have an MBA from Wharton and a highly discriminating analytical style. After lunching with her I plunged into learning more about the home builders and the mortgage market and came away wanting to move to Canada.

- My analysis of the homebuilding market and the overall housing market put a recovery in 2011. Wall Street had a turnaround happening in 2008.
- I found the home builders were going to take hits on multiple fronts—a gigantic falloff in operating profits, the write down of properties falling value, both houses and raw land; losses on mortgages they were holding that they could not offload; and problems financing their operations—they all lived on short-term commercial loans to finance activities. And all of this was available from, you guessed it, the Internet beginning with Yahoo! Finance.
- I had a dozen choices, and I focused on companies most exposed to the death of the subprime market—first-time buyers of starter homes—and to saturated markets including south Florida, Las Vegas, and California.
- I also picked up some ideas about regional banks exposed to problems with home sales, homebuilding, and home mortgages and selected a couple worth shorting.
- I checked the charts and got a bit nervous. These stocks were already down as much as 50 percent and had strong support at certain price levels. The number of shares held short was large and growing—potential positions could get hit by short squeezes. I weighted the indicators and then looked again at fundamentals and felt the terrible weakness in these companies would, or should, overcome these technical issues.
- Time to go short—and I put together a basket of choices including two regional banks—a segment trade using puts on individual equities. This basket also included collateral trades. At one time or another in 2007 or 2008 it held home builders; two regional banks; building suppliers; retail building suppliers such as Home Depot; and an international money transfer company, seeing a screeching end

to growth in money transfers from both legal and undocumented workers in the construction sector.

For the most part these positions did extremely well. They are proof you can play a segment with a basket of individual names rather than an ETF. This basket played out as follows:

- I recommended a total of 41 positions with the typical return of 62 percent.
- The first 29 positions had 27 winners return slightly more than 100 percent on average—and if you want to get a good laugh, the only two losers were two different positions in Countrywide Financial, the poster child of the subprime mortgage crisis.
- I had only two winners in my last 12 recommendations—most of these were blown up in two technical rallies and never recovered.

After the initial flurry of recommendations—they began on February 23, 2007—I created this large number of recommendations as I was now treating this entire segment as one giant trading pool of more than 30 publicly held companies. While the story never changed—home prices will continue to fall deeper and longer than Street expectations—my strategies changed over time based on the Street, technical rallies, and the prices of puts. I will skip a discussion of how I moved from one set of positions to another and will focus on the questions asked by my subscribers (in e-mail) and the problems that occasionally came up with these positions.

Why these names? The selection was initially based on weakening demand; it then moved toward the companies that were financially the weakest and with the highest probability of going under, which is where it stands at present.

Why recommend such volatile stocks? My analysis of the home builders was built on top of my view of the housing market, which in turn was built on forecasts for home prices. And my view was far more pessimistic than Wall Street's—I had a contrary view to their dates for a housing recovery—I saw this happening in late 2011/ early 2012, the Street was calling for a bottom in housing prices in 2010. My view was grounded on data—mortgage and home inventory data—and I saw another leg down coming. This belief was strong enough, a rarity, for me to downplay technical indicators and simply tell subs to gut out the volatility. This was the only position(s) I have ever recommended where the data was so strong I felt compelled to ignore volatility and downplay technical indicators.

Lesson Learned: You can successfully short a segment by building many positions and managing them aggressively. A benefit of this approach is you develop knowledge of that segment that enables you to ride out volatility and not confuse it with risk.

Conclusion

Not all trades are made alike, but most of them, the majority of them, can be successful if they are chosen and managed properly to profitability. The key is making decisions based on fundamentals— too much competition, tapped out customers, and falling margins at Ruby Tuesday; too many lousy mortgages at Bear; too many houses in inventory and too many foreclosures down the road for the home builders. Build the trades around and on top of these fundamentals, and manage them to make as much as you can but not all that you can.

Q&A

Q1. When you rolled Ruby Tuesday, did you tell your subscribers to press?

No. Many of them do anyway. I prefer to be conservative when providing day-to-day recommendations to people who may be less schooled in managing positions than people reading this book. My first instinct is to do no harm and I always recommend that when people roll a position they take their profits off the table.

Q2. Do you feel like you made a mistake by calling off the Bear trade just one trading day before the stock went from $25 and change to $2?

If the position had given my subs a 40 percent gain I would have to say yes—but with a 287 percent gain, no way. There was too much money on the table and no one could have anticipated Bear would be sold over the weekend for about the cost of the New York Yankees payroll—with the backing of the Fed.

(Continued)

Q3. When you selected individual home builders did you have concerns they were already down so much from their yearly highs?

Not as much as I should. I would not call it an oversight but a conscious decision that technical traders would only support brief rallies and there were not enough idiot bottom fishers to form a real floor for these stocks. These positions made a lot of money—several times—but were very difficult to manage. As I write this, some home builders have greater than 70 percent of their float held short and almost any news, good or bad, is followed by a short covering rally. This has been the case since January 2008 and can exhaust one's ability to properly manage a position.

Rules

- If the fundamentals hold, keep pushing, press on, and protect your capital as you see fit. But keep going for home runs when profits are coming your way.
- Be a pig but not a stupid one—in the face of chaos, take profits and a deep breath before doing anything new like rolling or pressing a position.
- You can successfully short a segment by building many positions and managing them aggressively. A benefit of this approach is you develop knowledge of that segment that enables you to ride out volatility and not confuse it with risk.

Glossary

ADRs   An ADR is an acronym for an American Depositary Receipt. An ADR is a proxy or representation of shares of a foreign company and trade in U.S. markets. Many foreign companies trade on U.S. exchanges in the form of ADRs and they are priced in U.S. dollars, trade like stocks, pay dividends, and some have call options. ADRs are issued by a U.S.-based depository bank.

analyst   Analysts are financial professionals with expertise in analyzing companies and/or investment instruments, offering clients or the public recommendations on how to deal with a specific security, typically buy it, hold it, or sell it. Also known as a financial analyst or security analyst. They are employed by investment banks, brokerage firms, investment advisors, or mutual funds.

Ask   This is the price a seller of a stock option or other investment instrument is willing to accept to complete a sale. The Ask is also called the "offer price."

asset   Any liquid or illiquid resource—it could be cash, bonds, loans, real estate, and other hard assets—that has a value. Assets are the basis of earnings at banks.

asset allocation   Asset allocation refers to how investors split their portfolios into different classes of investments, such as domestic stocks, bonds, international stocks, options, and so on.

average down   This is the method of buying stocks or options that entails buying more shares at a lower price than the price of the first purchase.

balance sheet   This is a company's financial statement—governed by accounting rules, what are called generally accepted accounting principles, as well as SEC and other government regulations. The balance sheet provides a window or snapshot into the assets, debts, and net worth of a company on a certain date.

bear market   A bear market is a meaningful decline in the prices of stocks, a commodity, bonds, or other investment instruments. A fairly well-accepted quantitative definition of a bear market is a price decline of 20 percent or more over at least an 8- to 10-week period.

beta   This is the measure of a stock's (or other security) volatility in comparison to the market and is one indicator of the riskiness of the stock. A beta equal to 1 means that the stock will trade as the market trades. A beta of less than 1 means it is less volatile than the market as a whole; greater than 1 means more volatile than the market. A beta of 1.5 means a stock is 50 percent more volatile than the market.

bid   This is the price or offer made by an investor to buy a stock or option or other security.

big cap stock   This is slang for a company with a market capitalization of between $10 billion and $200 billion.

binary event   An event that will drive a stock up or down such as an FDA approval or disapproval of a new drug.

Black–Scholes   This is a quantitative model commonly used to price options on stocks.

book value   This is an accounting concept that is the value of an asset, in this case a company, based on its accumulated assets, the value being calculated based on the original cost of the assets less depreciation, amortization, or impairment costs made against the asset. A subset is tangible book value.

bottom   This is the lowest price reached by a stock or other financial instrument in a given time period that is then followed by a steady increase. When a stock has hit bottom it has reached a low point and is typically about to enter an upward trend.

call contract   A contract that gives the buyer the right to buy 100 shares of a stock or other security at a fixed price at or before a date in the future.

capital   Your financial assets, including cash. Investment capital is the asset you invest or trade.

capital controls   Government regulations that prohibit or regulate the outflow or inflow of investment capital into or out of a country.

capital inflows   The term used to categorize the movement of investment capital into a country.

cash flow   This is the amount of cash generated by a company—or used if it is negative—during a specific time period. Cash flow is calculated by adding noncash charges to the net income or profits of a company after taxes.

catalyst   Something—an event, a piece of news—that prompts a stock to move in either direction.

ceiling   The term for a "top" for a stock or equity—typically when a stock hits a ceiling it then trades down or if it breaks through it establishes a new technical pattern for the stock.

commodities   Raw or other materials that range from oil to orange juice—in the context of investing and trading, commodities are materials and goods where futures contracts exist and can be traded.

consensus estimates/expectations   This is the average of the estimates provided by Wall Street analysts for earnings, revenues, and other financial metrics for a specific company.

contracts outstanding   This is the number of call or put contracts written for a specific equity or security.

covered call   This is a call contract written with the seller of the call owning the stock and being able to deliver it if she is "called" out of the stock.

cover a position   To cover is to buy the stock required to fulfill an obligation, either a call or to repay borrowed shares.

credit spread   A trading tactic where the trader sells a higher premium option and buys a lower premium option on the same underlying security.

days to cover   The number of days for all traders with a short position to cover their positions, calculated by dividing the number of shares held short by the average daily trading volume.

dividend   Monies paid to shareholders by a company on a per share basis.

double-short ETF   An ETF that moves in an inverse relationship to the movement of an index or market segment by a factor of 2 to 1—for every dollar a market index goes down, the double-short ETF goes up $2.

dumping shares   This term typically means the quick sale of shares by short sellers once they have borrowed these shares.

early sale   This occurs when the actual owner of borrowed shares asks for the borrowed shares back and sells these shares.

earnings   Profits.

EBITDA   Earnings before interest, taxes, depreciation, and amortization is a nonstandard or non-GAAP measure of a company's performance and profitability.

emerging markets   These are markets in lesser developed economies such as China, Russia, Brazil, and India.

entry point   This is the first price a trader or investor pays for an equity in options when establishing a position.

exchange traded fund   This is a fund that tracks an index or industry segment and is bought and sold like a stock. ETFs that track indices have components that reflect as closely as possible the underlying index. They are passive—the contribution of each component mirrors the index and is not changed due to market conditions.

expiration   This is the last date an option contract can be exercised; an option contract expires worthless if not exercised by the expiration date.

float   The number of shares available to trade.

floor   Another term for bottom.

fundamental analysis   A technique for evaluating a company and its stock based on the financial performance and other data about the company itself independent of the behavior of the stock or the market.

futures contracts   In the commodities market—and for certain indices—these are contracts that pledge the seller to deliver the actual goods, or basket of stocks, to the buyer at a certain date and price in the future.

income stocks   Stocks that have relatively high dividends as an integral part of the company's business model, not as a short-term tactic to attract shareholders.

institutional investor   An investor such as a mutual fund, large hedge fund, pension fund, and other organization with large pools of investment capital.

in the money   The term used to describe an option contract that is trading above (a call) or below (a put) its strike price. A $20 put contract on a stock trading for $17 dollars would be said to be in the money.

intrinsic or core value   This is the value of an option as measured by how much it is in the money. With call contracts, the core value is the difference between the underlying stock's price and the strike price of the option. With put contracts, the core or intrinsic value is the difference between the strike price and the underlying stock price.

LEAPS (Long-term Equity AnticiPation Securities)   These are longer-term puts or calls that can have expiration dates as far out as two years.

limit order   This is an order to buy or sell a set number of shares or contracts at a specified price or better. These orders can be time limited.

liquidity   A term that describes the ease, based on trading volume, with which a stock or other security can be traded without disturbing the price of that security.

locate   This is the activity by a broker to find shares a short seller wants to borrow.

margin call   When a stock or other position is created using margin loans, this is the request by the brokerage house for more funds from the investor, typically prompted by a decline in the value of positions in the investors' accounts.

margin interest   The interest paid in a margin account for funds borrowed by an investor.

market cap   Market cap or capitalization is the price of a company's shares multiplied by the number of shares outstanding.

market cap weighted index   An index that reflects the total market capitalization of all its components, such as the NASDAQ.

market order   An order to buy an equity or other security at the price set by the market.

Mike Tyson   Heavyweight boxing champ known for tattoos, ear biting, and the great insight: "everyone has a plan until they get punched in the face."

momentum indicator   A technical metric that measures how fast—the rate of acceleration—a stock or option is moving up or down.

money flow   This metric is determined by taking the average of a stock's high, low, and closing prices in a given day and then multiplying that figure by the number of shares traded.

moving average   A technical metric that shows a normalized view of the trend in a stock price. For example, if a 50-day moving average was $50, and the stock suddenly trades for $100 on the next day, the moving average would climb 2 percent or become $51.

naked calls   The sale of a call option without owning the underlying stock. The most aggressive form of shorting may be the sale of naked calls—you sell people the right to buy a stock at a price in the future and you don't own the stock because you are assuming the price of the stock will be less than the price in the call contract. This is a common, and legal, practice among many aggressive traders looking to short thinly traded stocks with hard-to-find shares to short.

naked shorting   The shorting of a stock without actually borrowing and selling the shares what the SEC calls affirmatively determined to exist. This practice is illegal.

NASDAQ   The National Association of Securities Dealers Automated Quotation—a stock market with all trading being done electronically and no central exchange.

option premium   The amount an option buyer pays for a call or put.

out of the money   The term used to describe an option contract that is trading below (a call) or above (a put) its strike price. A $20 put contract on a stock trading for $25 dollars would be said to be out of the money.

overweight   A position that is larger than the average position in a portfolio.

paired trade   A trade where an investor goes long one company and short another based on their relationship to each other in the real world.

press   To increase the size of a position that is working and profitable.

price-weighted index   A market index such as the Dow Jones whose components are all weighted by the price of their shares, not their market capitalization.

put   An option contract that gives the buyer of the put the right to sell a specified number of shares, 100 per contract, at a specific price on or before the put's expiration date.

put/call ratio   The ratio of put contracts outstanding to call contracts outstanding.

put contract   A put is an option contract that gives the buyer of the put the right to sell a specified number of shares, 100 per contract, at a specific price on or before the put's expiration date.

REIT   A Real Estate Investment Trust, an equity with special tax treatment—it avoids double taxation of profits and dividends—if it passes 90 percent of profits through to investors in the form of dividends.

relative value   The value of a company, based on any one of a number of financial metrics, such as price/earnings ratios, compared to the average of its industry or market segment.

rolling   This is a tactic where a trader closes a put position in a company and opens another put position in the same company at a different price and/or different strike price.

secular bear market   A bear market that is seen to last for a period longer than three to six months and within which there may be upswings in the market that are temporary.

sell stop   This is a predetermined price that an investor gives to a broker or enters into an online brokerage account to trigger an automatic sale of a stock or option.

shares outstanding   The number of shares issued by a company.

short covering rally   A run-up in a stock based on short sellers buying the stock to repay borrowed shares.

short ETF   An ETF that moves in an inverse relationship to the movement of an index or market segment. Also known as an inverse ETF.

short squeeze   This is an extreme example of a short covering rally where prices spike up as borrowers of the stock bid ever higher prices to obtain shares to cover their positions.

spread   The difference between the Ask and the Bid price for a stock, option, or other security.

stop loss   This is another term for a sell stop.

strike price   This is the price that gives the buyer of a call the right to buy the stock or a buyer of a put the right to sell the stock.

technical analysis   This is a set of techniques that analyzes the behavior of an individual security or a market based on the pattern of trading.

time decay   This is the ratio of the change in the price of an option to the movement of time as the option approaches its expiration date.

time stop   This is a date an investor creates to examine or close a position, typically used when managing options positions.

time value   This is the component of the option premium that is based on amount of time left before the option expires.

trading platform   Software, either on a computer or a website, which enables traders to analyze securities and trading tactics and execute trades.

trailing sell stop   This variant of a sell stop is used for profitable positions. The sell stop trails the price of the stock or option, often as a percentage below the most recent price of the position.

uptick rule   The discontinued government rule that mandates that a short sale may only occur at a price above the last sale price or at the last sale price if that price was higher than the previous price.

vega   This is the change in price of an option compared to a 1 percent change in the volatility of that option. The vega of an option can change if the option becomes more volatile even if the underlying stock price does not change.

volatility   This is the measure of how much a stock or option rises and falls within a specified length of time. Volatility is a key component in the pricing of put options.

whisper numbers   The quiet or hidden expectations of traders on Wall Street for a company's earnings that are often different than published estimates by analysts.

About the Author

Michael Shulman is the editor of *ChangeWave Shorts*, an investment and trading service providing advice to individuals and professionals. In both 2007 and 2008 Mr. Shulman saw returns greater than 50 percent, on average, for the positions he recommended in this service. He has run several other ChangeWave services, including a letter on biotech and the company's institutional research service, ChangeWave Insight.

Michael has had an eclectic career, buying his first stock in 1978, trading his first option in 1987, and never looking back. A graduate of Georgetown University with a degree in philosophy, he has always found himself somewhere a bit in front of others—working on President Jimmy Carter's National Energy Plan (while still a senior in college), in Silicon Valley for a company called Mindset (one of 49 personal computer companies that existed at the time), in the computer group of AT&T, and, before entering the financial industry, as the founder and CEO of an Internet company. He has also served on the board of a venture capital fund and various advisory boards and been published in a variety of publications ranging from the *Los Angeles Times* to The Motley Fool. Michael has also appeared frequently on Fox Business and CNBC. He is now working hard to find a publisher for two financial thrillers related to—you guessed it—the shorting of stocks.

Michael currently resides in Maryland, is the husband of former ABC News correspondent Jackie Judd, and, as his subscribers well know, continues to be, on a daily basis, harangued about anything and everything by the two finest men he has ever met, his twin teenage sons.

Index